PRAISE
PLANET V

"A loving, gracious invitation to a land that is ever so difficult to traverse."

> – Geneen Roth, author of the #1 *New York Times* bestseller, *Women Food and God* and her most recent book, *This Messy Magnificent Life*

"*Notes from Planet Widow* is no less than a guidebook for handling grief. Any kind of deep grief. There's nothing precious or saccharine in the wisdom Gwen offers. She offers the truth, which happens to be just as painful as it is filled with grace. She models a beautiful way forward."

> –Kelley Weber, Spiritual Director, Aspiralspace.com

"*Notes from Planet Widow* is written in an informal style that is filled with rich descriptive metaphors. Reading this book is to have a gentle conversation with Gwen. She is transparent in her coming to terms with the loss of her husband, Jack. The documentation of her journey provides the reader practical information, resources, and illustrations that serve as a graceful guide through the angst, pain, and loneliness of the loss of a love."

> –Jackson Rainer, Ph.D., ABPP, Board Certified Clinical Psychologist, psychotherapist, educator, author, and expert in the areas of grief and bereavement, and end of life and palliative care.

"In *Notes from Planet Widow*, author Gwen Suesse reflects on her experience with grief after the sudden death of her husband, Jack. Using the lens of deep grief, she takes us through her experiences with hope, anger, loneliness, and myriad other emotions as illustrated by poignant memories and reflections on her own moments of deep meaning-making after loss. Through shifting perspectives and embracing the present, the author found ways to thrive and find joy again. From there, she shows us not necessarily one right way—because there isn't only one right way—but a path from which we can learn and tools to explore along the way."

   –Tamara Beachum, Grief Educator

"This insightful work narrates Gwen's journey of grief and grace in widowhood. Quoting myriad writers, sages, philosophers, poets, and more, it blazes with personal and universal understandings... As a stand-alone, the Resources section at the end is an invaluable tool to help readers pursue their own journeys of self-compassion and acceptance."

   –Sara J. Glerum, beatstalkingtomyself.com

"This book is deep, curious, and full of wonder... It is a gifted piece of writing.... sometimes difficult yet elevating to read. Wise and wonderful."

   –Leigh Steiner, Ph.D., Former Illinois Commissioner of Mental Health

Notes from Planet Widow

ALSO BY GWEN SUESSE

*Womansong: Balance and
Harmony in a Feminine Key*
(2010)

Notes from Planet Widow

Finding my way after loss.

GWEN SUESSE

Cantando
Press

Notes from Planet Widow: Finding My Way After Loss
©2024, Gwen Suesse. All rights reserved.
Published by Cantando Press, Tryon, North Carolina

ISBN: 979-8-9897552-1-9 (paperback)
ISBN: 979-8-9897552-0-2 (eBook)
Library of Congress Control Number: 2024908586

gwensuesseauthor.com

Publication managed by AuthorImprints.com

For All Who Mourn:
May They Find Comfort.

My hope must take a different form
than the one I had shaped for it.

~ *David Whyte*

TABLE OF CONTENTS

INTRODUCTION

When you have come to the edge
of all the light you know,
Into the darkness of the unknown,

Faith is knowing that one of two things will happen.

There will be something solid to stand on,

Or you will be taught how to fly.

~ Patrick Overton

THE FACT that I am writing this introduction is proof that people can and do survive loss. When loss hit me, I wasn't sure I'd live through it, but I did, and you will, too.

Loss is as old as humankind. And human beings have evolved to be able to endure it, to survive it, and even thrive in its wake. That's the good news.

The bad news—might as well be honest, right from the start—is that we never get over it. Our lives are forever altered. There are times when we don't think we *can* endure the loss, when we're not sure we even want to.

Although my story unfolds in terms of widowhood, the feelings and situations I have experienced (and am still experiencing) with this seismic shift seem remarkably similar across all forms of loss, whether sparked by the death of a spouse, parent, child, or beloved friend; or the loss of a job, a family, a home, or a life irreversibly altered by illness. Loss of any kind is disorienting. It erases the illusion of having control over the arc of our lives. It guts our sense of normalcy. It undermines security and rips asunder our expectations.

From the start, I longed to put grief in my rearview mirror, but great loss is an abiding ache that defies eradication. Like salt in the sea, some memories never leave our bones. They become part of us, so we must learn how to carry them. Thrust on a journey I didn't anticipate and certainly didn't choose, the only choice remaining was how I'd respond. Would I pursue a path of reintegration or remain in the parking lot of despair?

I chose to claw my way out of that parking lot. I chose to keep moving.

My beloved husband died when I was sixty-two, young enough to feel like any such loss, while statistically likely, was years away. Without warning that mindset evaporated. Jack was gone. His death occurred just thirteen days after initial symptoms of shortness of breath. Instantaneously, the ground beneath me disappeared and I landed on "Planet Widow."

I had to figure out how to navigate without a road map.

Søren Kierkegaard observed that life can only be understood backwards, although it must be lived forwards. I found "living forwards" to be fraught with one roadblock or pothole after another: the oppressing presence of absence. The unfathomable sorrow of a house that echoes with the silence of having no one to talk to. Brewing coffee in the morning and realizing only half as much is needed. Trying to start the generator during a power failure and needing to call the electrician because I failed to flick one critical switch. Electrically controlled clerestory windows that opened by themselves. (Really! Turns out the wind had stripped the gears, meaning that outside air pressure could cause them to open, but I thought I was losing my mind.) Legal issues with all the exacting protocols they entail. Our corgi, Daisy, knowing somehow that Jack was gone and behaving badly to punish me for that by failing to wait to go outside to do what dogs do when she never ever had "accidents" prior to this time. One uncontrollable thing after another, day after day after day.

So many details were demanding expertise, attention, and energy at a time when my fuel gauge was already running on empty, my knuckles already white from desperately clutching the steering wheel.

Desperate to find direction, I did what I always do: I wrote.

I wrote, hoping that "thinking on paper" would show me my path as it has done so often over my lifetime. Looking back over journal entries years later, a path of breadcrumbs had emerged, subtly and slowly, one tiny morsel at a time. Easily overlooked individually, but as they accumulated, a way forward came into focus and gathered energy.

To be clear, no magic formula for obliterating sadness, loneliness, and despair magically appeared along the way. However, even in the midst of darkest gloom, acts of kindness, dapples of light, scraps of humor, and smidgens of hope beckoned to me from the distance, coaxing me forward.

This is my story, colored by my specific circumstances, but its revelations and lessons can, I believe, be applied to a broad spectrum of loss experiences.

Introduction

If these musings sound preachy, they probably are. They were written for a congregation of *one,* that one being me. I wrote what I needed to hear. I share these thoughts because they helped me, and I hope they might help you, too.

In the end, only three things matter:

~How much you loved.

~How gently you lived.

~How gracefully you let go of

Things not meant for you.

~ Buddha

CHAPTER ONE

HARD LANDING

To fully grasp the magnitude of what you've lost requires the experience of having to do without it.

~ Gail Godwin

PLANET WIDOW

PLANET WIDOW. A desolate, hostile land. Bleak. Unfamiliar. Foreign. So far away until suddenly it was not; until, like Dorothy, picked up and deposited in Oz by a tornado, I found myself plunked down in a strange barren landscape, overwhelmed by unrecognizable terrain. I was awash in grief, heartache, and disorientation. How could I navigate this unknown land? How could I find my way forward when there was only half of me left to do that?

All I could see was grayness, everywhere grayness, obscured with apparitions of death, visions of loss, and specters of being alone pockmarking the landscape.

For Dorothy, there was a yellow brick road. I saw no roads of any kind or color. No way forward and no safe haven. I was consumed by desolation, loneliness, and cold fear.

That stark, terrifying, hard landing happened years ago. In time the edges softened, the landscape came into focus, and colors reemerged. It is a strange truth that human beings are endlessly adaptable, even when we don't want to be. We become inured to our situations in spite of ourselves. Surviving grief is as old as humankind. Life does go on. Somehow, we manage to "continue to continue," as the Simon & Garfunkel song goes.

Initial paralysis slowly morphed into a truce of sorts with this new terrain. Seeing no alternative, I reluctantly embarked on a messy, disorganized, nonlinear process steeped in a brew of grief, heartache, self-doubt, and gut-wrenching loneliness. This process entailed false starts, full stops, unexpected roadblocks, unforeseeable hurdles, periodic rebellions, hand-wringing insecurities, agonizing uncertainties, and all other manner of obstacles and challenges. One day followed another. Somehow life went on.

What makes such transformation possible? Surely Grace—Grace, capital-G—that unmerited, mystical assistance that defies explanation, surely that was at work, carrying me when I could no longer carry myself, shifting my spirit when life had ebbed to its darkest moments, revealing glimmers of hope, difference, love, and possibility.

Examples spring to mind: A friend showing up with a plastic produce bucket full of ice and a bottle of wine. Omnipresent friends—each helping in their own signature way—through phone calls or emails or sharing books or splitting wood for my wood stove. Nature stunning me with her resilience and outrageous beauty as dappled sun sparkled through the trees and onto the stream next to my favorite hiking path, reminding me of Light, Hope, and Buoyancy, hinting that despite everything, joy can still be found. Grace in plain sight alongside the grief, coaxing me inch by excruciating inch to stop staring at closed doors and turn to windows open with possibilities.

If Grace ignites the engine of transformation, Curiosity is the fuel that feeds it and sustains its forward motion. When I began to look for the messages that were riding quietly in tandem alongside my circumstances and emotions, my spirit began to shift, one slow cog in the gearbox at a time. I didn't know where I was headed, but somehow, I was not as stuck as I was before curiosity came along.

Questions are what give Curiosity structure, converting vague, unshaped prospects into specific inquiries. What am I failing to notice? What one little thing can I try doing a little differently? Curiosity helps us investigate possibilities vicariously. We get to try things on, see what fits, figuratively dipping a toe into the water before taking a plunge.

Questions, it turns out, provide the alchemy for transformation.

The way forward, therefore, is deceptively simple, although challenging to execute: just keep formulating questions and follow their trail to see where they lead. Be open. Be inquisitive. Stay as wide awake as you can, with radar fine-tuned to pick up every blip of possibility. As the lovely, little painting on the wall of my study says, "The opportunity that God sends does not wake up him who is asleep."

I'm getting ahead of myself in the interest of offering a kernel of hope at the outset. Things do get better if we simply hang on, however tentatively. It is possible not only to survive but to thrive if we allow ourselves to surrender to the depths of grief and dare to forge our way forward, one painful step at a time.

The emergence of the welcome talismans of Grace, Curiosity, and Questions cannot come before enduring a long, lonely journey. Arrive, however, they did. They came, but on their schedule, not mine. Little by little, these good companions blossomed and led me gently onward.

Slowly, I wrestled my way forward. Slowly, the lay of the land came into focus. Slowly, a new equilibrium took hold—and I began to live again.

CHAPTER TWO

GETTING THE LAY OF THE LAND

You can't use an old map to
explore a new world.

~ *Albert Einstein*

THE JOURNEY BEGINS

DAY 10 of life after Jack. His memorial service feels like a distant memory. My son and daughter have gone back to their lives. I awake to a silent, empty house. (Is it still a home?) The silence is deafening, ominous, heavy. Jack's absence is a looming presence. Time itself feels different, the hours longer and the days a blur, with nothing to anchor me and keep me tethered. I am adrift, sad beyond measure, and frightened. How will I manage this?

The slog begins. Everything—every single thing!—is altered, from making morning coffee (no need to make six cups anymore) to taking out the garbage (all those bailiwicks that we divided now belong solely to me) to what to do with solo evenings. (No more after-dinner chitchats.)

❊   ❊   ❊

There I was, a stranger in a strange land, the talismans of Grace, Curiosity, and Questions undiscovered at this point, not yet within sight to guide me. I didn't know what to do, but I knew I needed to hold myself together. The only thing that occurred to me was to apply Discipline, capital-D Discipline. Get a grip, I told myself! Don't go to bed too early. (Or too late.) Don't get up too early. (Or

too late.) Eat well. (Not too much. Not too little.)
Don't drown sorrows in glasses of wine. (Surely
one glass is allowed?) Exercise, never missing a day.
Do the damn paperwork. Be friendly to others.
Say "yes" to everything that is remotely promising.
Offend no one. Don't wear out your welcome with
your friends. Save your calls for desperation. (Yeah.
A really dumb idea to ration times to reach out
to others.)

Slowly, the days ticked by. I began to notice that
grief *flows.* There were times when I thought I
couldn't last another ten minutes, let alone get to
tomorrow. Yet ten minutes later, there I still was,
grief not gone, but the intense wave somewhat
dissipated, bearable in a way it had not been
moments ago. Apparently, grief was not going to
kill me.

Hours turned into days, days into weeks, and
weeks into months. I read everything I could find
about dealing with grief. Understanding everything
may change nothing, but it's a start. At least I felt
like I was trying. I got a counselor. I wrote. My
journal became my coping buddy because I needed
"someone" to talk to. The pages were always there
for me, ready to "listen," often yielding an inkling of
insight or a scrap of comfort.

An amorphous Presence held me. It would be a
while before I could recognize that presence was

Grace—the manifestation of infinite unconditional love—which silently, steadfastly held me, asking nothing in return.

That pretty much sums up the beginning.

* * *

The next period was a dark one. I woke up one day realizing—duh!—that I could not outlast this situation. *I would be living without Jack not for some undefined period but for the rest of my life.* The rest of my life! How could I possibly do that? I was in way over my head. I was out of gas, exhausted, more scared than ever, even, at times, wishing I were dead. My skin prickled with angst. I paced aimlessly. Either my heart was racing, or I was enervated and leaden with lethargy, alternately unable to sit still and unable to move. I couldn't figure out what to do or where to go, subconsciously imagining I could dispel this chaotic terror if I did something or went somewhere. Alas, whatever you do, wherever you go, there you are. The baggage is attached.

I hit bottom. I needed a new plan.

"Bottom" is a scary place to be, but clarity was born from that descent. I was in the iron grip of hubris, trying to deal with my pain entirely by myself. I wanted to be strong—somehow I had come to equate loving my husband enough with being strong enough to be a "model widow," whatever that might look like. The irony, of course, is that all my high-mindedness served only to make things harder.

The truism holds: when you hit bottom, there's nowhere to go but up. I made an appointment with my doctor and asked for help. I was ashamed to need medication but got beyond that once I understood that I had a chemical imbalance caused by extreme stress. A friend told me that antidepressants don't solve anything, but they do keep you out of the subbasement of despair. They help level things out, and that was what I needed to break the cycle of incapacitating desolation.

After a few weeks on medication, a nascent stability took hold. I began to get a grip and feel motivated to figure out how to move forward. From my journal:

What I'm feeling this morning is immense relief, the relief of realizing that this isn't about failure or strength. I hereby take myself off the hook. This is like a pile of blankets that have been heaped on top of each other (and on me) until reaching the critical tipping point of suffocation. Grief. Shock. Logistics. And loneliness, Oh, dear God, the loneliness. I can't breathe. I'm plumb out of "trying harder." I have been trying so hard, for so long, to be "strong." I give up.

I have decided to redefine "strong." I AM strong, dammit! Sinuous. My strength is embedded in a thousand ways, in a thousand threads that are intertwined in complicated but durable ways. But even "strong" needs maintenance, so I'm getting some. Not to mention that "honest strength" knows when to ask for help.

My initial plan of Discipline, capital-D, while all good and fine, had carried me just so far. I'd been patching myself together under the unconscious, mistaken impression that all I needed to do was to try harder, to hang on long enough for the pain to dissipate. As in "go away." Talk about magical thinking! Feelings do not miraculously disappear, no matter how long one waits. Release comes only after fully reckoning with them.

I was trying to solve the wrong problem.

My pain came from loss. Loss does not dissipate. If anything, it accrues. Only eradication of the cause would eradicate the pain, and that was not possible. I needed to figure out how to incorporate my loss into a bigger picture, not obliterate it. I needed to find a whole new way of looking at my life. The only way around would be *through*—to become willing to acknowledge and wrestle with my pain and ultimately alchemize it into a new way of being so that, like forged steel, I would emerge stronger for the process endured.

Having discovered a new way to view my challenge, I was ready to proceed. But how? With all this barren landscape, how could I know where to step?

BABY STEPS

ZERISSENHEIT IS one of those German words that means so much more than its literal translation; in this case, brokenness, disunity, torn-apartness. I was awash in it, churning turbulently in a wild array of thoughts and ideas. I ricocheted like a tightly wound pendulum, swinging from inklings that I could find my way to utter terror that I could not, and thinking of all sorts of other possibilities in between. I was in a constant state of über-vigilance, always on guard, braced to survive.

Looking over the landscape, I stuck out a tentative toe anywhere and at anything that looked like it might be helpful. That point there: Is it firm? Will it hold me? Will it help? Or maybe over there ... or there ...

The pendulum needed to settle a bit. I needed to stop clutching at straws, slow down, breathe, and cut myself some slack. Above all, I needed to stop expecting instant results.

The Discipline I applied without mercy in the early days was useful, but I had carried it too far, making a crutch of it. I was using self-control to bypass grief. The result was exhaustion. Inner chatter of self-flagellation went on and on: Why didn't I feel better?

Why didn't I do better? What was the matter with me? Why couldn't I just buck up and get a grip?

This constant litany of criticisms and self-recriminations was like acid eating away my soul.

One day I came across John O'Donohue's *To Bless the Space Between Us: A Book of Blessings.* In "For the Interim Time," he describes what it's like to be in a time when everything you've known has disappeared, yet no direction has yet come into being. "The old is not old enough to have died away; the new is still too young to be born . . ."

That's it—the perfect description of Planet Widow. O'Donohue goes on to encourage patience saying, "It is difficult and slow to become new . . ."

In one sense, words change nothing; in another, they tilt one's world on a new axis instantaneously. I wanted to feel better *now.* O'Donohue's wise and comforting message implied that my time frame needed adjusting. My frenzied sense of failure de-escalated with the reminder that change takes time. It sounds banal and obvious but lost in my sea of grief, I needed that nudge. I needed to know I was in company with legions of grievers, and, like them, was limping along and doing the best I could, and that that was "good enough." I could do my part but only time could do the rest.

"Breathe . . ." says C.S. Lewis. "This is just a chapter, it's not the whole story."

It was a call to surrender, a first baby step in a new direction.

PERSPECTIVE IS IMPORTANT

Much of dealing with death and grieving is
about embracing the mystery of life rather than
thinking we need to have answers for it all.

~ Cath Duncan

THE WORK of author and coach Jamie Smart
illuminates the interrelationships among time,
thinking, and how understanding something deeply
can change one's relation to it. Often we default to
framing our thoughts in our "old" language, using
outgrown ways of thinking, relying on obsolete
maps of our world. We seek answers to something
we can't yet, indeed if ever, know.

In an interview with Cath Duncan during the
Creative Grief Studio certification program, Smart
observed that

> *Our thinking always appears as though it's the
> reality... we get covered over with our habitual
> thinking... We live in a thought-generated reality
> moment to moment. Painful feelings aren't telling
> you about your future. They're telling you that your*

thinking has gone toxic in the moment... [you] think the bad feeling is telling [you] how real it is. But it's not. It's telling [you] how untrustworthy that vision is in the moment.

We can always have a fresh new thought, and fresh new thoughts come from the unknown. And when we have a fresh new thought, we're suddenly in a fresh new world... It's the unknowns that are the source of something that's going to be valuable, precious, and powerful to me going forward... The unknown is where the good things are. The unknown is where the good stuff comes from.

Smart goes on to say, "Who we are at the core of us is spirit, is energy, and there's nothing in this world that can harm who we really are."

O'Donohue reminds us to allow time. Smart counsels us to beware of couching new situations in outmoded viewpoints. The poet/philosopher David Whyte underscores this perspective when he asks if we can allow ourselves to "travel" without always being able to see the path ahead.

The roadless landscape ahead can be viewed in two ways: as terrifying in its lack of definition or as wide open with opportunity. We get to decide which way we will view it as we inch forward.

CHAPTER THREE

BREADCRUMBS APPEAR, ONE BY ONE

Hope
Hope has holes
in its pockets.
It leaves little
crumb trails
so that we,
when anxious,
can follow it.
Hope's secret:
it doesn't know
the destination—
it knows only
that all roads
begin with one
foot in front
of the other.

~ Rosemerry Wahtola Trommer

From *All the Honey* (Samara Press, 2023)
Used with permission of the author.

A GUIDING LIGHT

RECOGNIZE THIS right from the start: grief is a disorderly process. It lacks predictability. There are several theories about its stages or sequences, but in my experience, feelings, thoughts, and events jumble willy-nilly in a ferocious stew. There is no order, and the process careens this way and that way with wild abandon.

Helpful signs, messages, and inspirations are part of this mix. They show up within and around the chaos, usually unexpected, with no discernable pattern or logic. Sometimes, they are so subtle you don't immediately notice them. Sometimes, they come sooner than you can digest them, meaning you must grow into them. And sometimes, there is a long barren period of longing and emptiness before some glimmer comes to light.

In my case, the first helpful sign was my husband's voice. It showed up mere days after he died, and I was not ready for it.

I know, I know, this is woo-woo kind of stuff, embraced by some, scoffed at by others. Did I really hear Jack's voice or only imagine it? Was it wishful thinking or reality? Does it matter?

There are "thin place" times; times when we are more acutely aware of things just beyond the conscious level. Paranormal times. This was one of them, following several instances of things being different in my home. Drapes shut when I had not closed them. Objects inexplicably relocated to different places. Of course, my first thought was that I was losing it, out of control, and imagining things. And yet, I report what I experienced.

Walking through my living room, I suddenly heard Jack's voice. No mistaking it. *You know, Gwennie, you can't live without me the way you lived with me.* Hearing him stopped me cold. I looked up— somehow that seemed like the direction the voice was coming from—but after those few short words, only silence.

It was unnerving. I remember answering, *I know that! But I don't know how to live without you! I don't even know where to start.*

I didn't know how to process this unusual occurrence. Too overwhelming at the time, the experience was quickly shunted aside by my disorientation, fear, and disquietude. A seeming anomaly, it waited patiently in the mists until I was ready to hear it, able to accept it, and gather courage to embody it.

In the moment, his words felt harsh, like a recrimination. In retrospect, I see his message was a "portent": a prophetic indication granting me permission to do things differently. I needed this message because, oddly, in the early days after loss, any deviation from old patterns feels like disloyalty. Jack's message set a tone for learning to live again. It was too soon for me to be able to do that, but his words were a guiding light as time went by, like a lighthouse showing the way to a safe harbor.

GIFT OF FULL STOP

You wouldn't feel so stuck if you
could see the whole picture.

~ *Sandy Gingras*

EXPERIENCING LOSS is often accompanied by an inability to make decisions. The unfamiliar territory of changed circumstances is incapacitating. We just don't know what to do; it's a situation that feeds on itself, grinding us to a halt.

I remember this feeling all too well. Alarmed by torpor and inertia, I wondered how in the world I would ever be able to move forward when I seemed unable to make even the least little decisions.

Of course, I *was* making the "least little decisions." I got up in the morning. I made coffee. I got the mail. I did the little daily things that keep life going. There was forward motion. It just didn't feel significant enough because, subconsciously, I equated "making decisions" with feeling better. And I was desperate to feel better!

It turns out, however, that the uncomfortable feeling of grinding to a halt is a necessary part of reformulating our decision-making process. We aren't wired with switches to instantly change gears when our lives have been upended, magically helping us to make different choices. Changing our long-established ways of making decisions takes time. Before we can establish momentum in new directions, we must allow the old ways to come to an end. But this is hard because deep inside, we don't want them to end.

We need to stop. Full stop! Unwilling to do so on our own, Mother Nature steps in with her ironic gift of lethargy, like clicking the "force quit" icon on a hung computer. Incapacitation forces us to abandon our old ways in order to find new momentum.

At this point, our job is to give in and give up. Make the coffee, get the mail, but put off as many issues and decisions as possible to wait for another day. Rest. Breathe, knowing that this hiatus is exactly that: a temporary pause, not a permanent condition. Our spirits seek time to rejuvenate and reorient. We need to befriend them, not do battle with them.

Fallow time is a regenerative phase. Rest is required to foster healing and enable renewed energy and direction. "Let it be," sang John Lennon. "...
there is still a light that shines on me. Shine until tomorrow, let it be..."

FEEL WHAT YOU FEEL

(But don't expect to know what
that will be in advance!)

THE EARLY breadcrumbs were so obvious they could easily have been overlooked. Had I not paid attention to them, I would've remained stuck indefinitely. I couldn't think my way out of this, but I could commit to attending and befriending my needs instead of denying them and castigating myself. It was a start.

I began scanning my surroundings, putting one foot in front of the other, doggedly determined to *pay attention,* to see opportunities instead of roadblocks.

An acquaintance reached out to me with a lunch invitation, even though the only thing we had in common was our status as widows, both of us members of a club that no one wants to belong to.

Not one for chit-chat, she got right to her point: "Feel what you feel," she said. "That's the single best piece of advice I got."

This short phrase gave me the permission I needed to let my feelings flow instead of trying to create and control them. I wanted so badly to "do this thing right." My friend's message was that there is no right or wrong; there is just what you feel.

Having permission, however, is different than putting it into action. For those of us who are planners, it's challenging to stay real, to stay with what we're truly feeling. It's so easy, even tempting, to conjure a vision of what I wish I were feeling instead. The problem with conjuring an alternate reality is that it obscures the very things that I need to feel to move forward.

We can't *control* our feelings, and we can't know ahead of time what they will be. Our feelings simply are what they are. Given full voice, they can ride on through instead of tying us in knots. They're emotions. They need the *motion* part of that word to be helpful, but that doesn't come before allowing the feelings themselves.

Rumi's poem *The Guest House* (Jelaluddin Rumi, translation by Coleman Barks) suggests how we might begin. He encourages us to welcome whatever feelings and emotions show up—"Even if they're a crowd of sorrows"—because everything that comes to us "has been sent as a guide from beyond."

Rumi tells us to let go of our expectations. To give up on even *needing* to know. To consent to experiencing our feelings instead of trying to orchestrate them. He suggests that beyond our tribulations and blindness, there is an ultimate sense to things. Hang on, he seems to say. Trust that all will be well.

Feel without judging yourself for feeling. Whatever it is, disappointment or surprise, sadness or joy, envy or contentment, fear or relief—sit with it and in it. Then let it go on its way, making room for whatever will arrive in its wake. Keep moving.

~ Maggie Smith

ONE NEXT THING

LIVING ALONE after decades of living with someone else is startling, unnerving, disorienting, and frightening. The old ways of doing things no longer work.

The summer my husband died, instead of heading north for the summer together as we usually did, Jack went by himself first to complete a boat project. There wasn't enough room for both of us on board during this process, so for the first time I stayed behind, planning to join him three weeks later when the project would be complete.

Oh, the irony: I remember so well sending him off, almost gleeful at the prospect of having three solid weeks all to myself, blissfully unaware that my life as I knew it was about to end. I went merrily about my way, reading, writing, hiking, gardening— doing things I always did but with a sense of grand abandon, no schedule necessary, no thought to anything or anybody other than what I wanted to do in the moment. It was a lovely interlude.

In retrospect, it wasn't so much a "lovely interlude" as an ominous foreshadowing. All too soon I'd have nothing *but* time to myself. I did go north as planned. We were together again for a few short weeks, but then Jack was gone. Permanently gone.

In a way, it's a matter of perspective about the cooperation and consideration that's integral to a solid marriage: Jack never kept me from setting my own schedule or pursuing my own interests, but when you live with someone you love and respect, there is always a sense of awareness of where they are, what they're doing, and whether your comings and goings fit compatibly with theirs. It's not an obligation but a privilege, a cultivated and reassuring way of living together.

When you find yourself alone, however, that perspective must change. You must find a new centering principle, different routines, and new ways of doing things.

Gail Godwin's *Old Lovegood Girls* is a story involving widowhood. Godwin observes: "This she had learned from living alone. You fared best when you knew what you wanted to do next."

Notice that she says, "know what you want to do *next,*" not "know what you want to do with the rest of your life!"

Thus, when you feel yourself sinking, ask yourself: "What's next?" Any one thing from getting a quart of milk to reading a new novel to deliberately sitting still. Just keep doing "next." Big dreams are great, but it's the daily one-foot-in-front-of-the-other approach that holds you together, preserves you in this interim time.

Creating an intention, at least one for each day, gets you from that day to the next and then to the one after that. "Next things" begin to assemble themselves into new routines that lead the way as you invent a new modus operandi.

Decide on one next thing. Just one . . .

ASSEMBLE YOUR TEAM

THE CHALLENGES were practical as well as emotional and spiritual. So many things needed to be done—filling out paperwork, tackling financial matters, doing household maintenance, selling boats (yes, plural), closing a business, figuring out tax forms, answering questions, addressing legal issues, and on and on... Although I tried to focus on one thing at a time, the mere thought of all these challenges overwhelmed me, rendering me panicked and sleepless.

Just when I needed it most, another breadcrumb appeared in a morning reading:

> *It's not so much that we're afraid of change or so in love with the old ways, but it's that place in between we fear... It's like being between trapezes. It's Linus when his blanket is in the dryer. There's nothing to hold on to.*
>
> ~ Marilyn Ferguson

Ferguson's words paint a concrete image of the terrifying lack of groundedness that I felt. There is comfort, somehow, in having one's feelings accurately articulated, sensing that someone else has felt what I am feeling. Her words also hint at possible resolutions. Perhaps there was another trapeze headed in my direction, soon to be within reach. If not, most likely—my inference—there would be a safety net below to catch me if I fall.

Aha! A safety net. What might that look like?

That answer came from my kids. "Mom," they said, "you don't have to be able to do everything yourself. Assemble your team!"

And so, I did. I enlisted multiple helpers. My daughter coached me in learning how to use the software that organizes my finances. My son helped with selling and moving things. My financial advisor, as planned, was extra attentive during the transition phase. I found an accountant to help me settle Jack's business concerns. A close friend introduced me to a fabulous guy to help with household and yard chores. My lawyer suggested a tax preparer. Another good friend recommended the counselor who became my indispensable source of succor, objectivity, and wisdom. I learned to look for other outside experts as needed.

It was a big adjustment because Jack and I had always done pretty much everything on our own without much outside help. We had complementary strengths and skills. Between us, we could accomplish what we needed to mostly on our own.

Without his contributions, a new paradigm for putting my life together was required. It reminded me that while change is unsettling, awkward, and scary, it is not an insurmountable task if one is willing to ask for help.

As the wise Mr. Rogers said, "Look for the helpers."

THERE IS ALWAYS
A WAY—ALWAYS!

HELPERS. CHEERY thought. Are they *always* to be found? Is there *always* a solution, a remedy, a way out?

I believe there is. Maybe not the solution I had in mind, but there is always—*always*—a way forward, which was a lesson I learned in an unlikely place.

One Friday afternoon I decided to take some time off from chores and my legal slog and go plant shopping. I needed to replenish my deck pots. I decided to splurge by going to a nursery that while farther away had a greater selection of eye candy for enthusiastic gardeners.

I meandered in, out, and around their extensive grounds, up one path, down the next. At one point I found some hollies that seemed perfect for my needs. My cart was behind me. I was vaguely aware of a tow motor in the path, but I did not take in that its forks were extended at the level of my head. I picked up a pot, turned around to place it on my cart, and smacked into one of the forks, cutting my forehead open and somehow cutting one wrist as well.

Stunned, I brought my hand to my head to discover I was bleeding profusely. My first instinct was embarrassment. How could I be so stupid? Then reality set in. This wasn't about embarrassment; it was about crisis. I was alone, forty-five miles from home, bleeding, and in trouble with no one to help me, a widow's worst nightmare.

What was I going to do? Driving home didn't feel wise. (Good call: turns out I had a mild concussion.) Take an ambulance to the hospital? That seemed like an overreaction. I just wanted someone to be there for me, someone to take charge, figure out what to do, and help me do it.

And that's what happened. The nursery staff quickly noticed my predicament, took me into the break room, and found a cloth I could use to compress the bleeding. I was concerned that I was bothering them, tried to fade into the woodwork, which is hard to do when you're bleeding. The owner asked how he could help. ("Yeah," said my son. "He probably thought you were going to sue him.")

Agreeing with me that I shouldn't drive, he offered to drive me home and have one of his employees follow him, driving my car. I called a friend who said she'd be there when I arrived. She quickly whisked me to an urgent care facility where I was able to check in just before closing time. An hour later I was stitched up and ready to go.

The experience was a profound turning point for me. Calamities and misadventures will occur. There will be times when I will feel utterly alone and desperate, but perhaps a significant part of what's going on at such times is that I'm letting fear instead of trust run the show, believing in doom instead of believing that a way to deal with the problem will emerge.

Trust, said my bandaged self to my spirit. *Trust the generosity of the Universe. Dare to send out positive energy. It will attract that same energy in return. There will always be a way.*

ADAPT TO GET YOUR GROOVE BACK

---

*You know, sometimes it's the artist's task
to find out how much music you can
still make with what you have left.*

*~ Itzhak Perlman
(On finishing a concert with only three
strings on his violin after one snapped.)*

A FEELING of disempowerment often accompanies great loss as our sense of agency and control go up in smoke and evaporate on the horizon. Things just don't work the way they did before. *We* don't work the way we did before. We sense that something was done to us, something we were powerless to prevent and tend to equate that with having no power whatsoever.

Disempowerment and loss are not necessarily linked, but within the unruliness and disruption caused by great upheaval, it can feel like they are, resulting in a downward spiral of debilitating doubt, stunted ability to function, or, even worse, a sense of victimhood.

Absent the magic of a fairy's wand, the only available antidote is attitude. We may have lost significant amounts of control, but we haven't lost all of it. We must refuse to cede whatever remains. If only three strings remain on the violin, then that's what we'll play on. The music has not stopped, nor must we. Positive self-talk helps.

From my journal:

> *Things just "are." If difficult, heart-stopping things have come my way, so, too, have come ways to deal with those things. I'm not less competent, I just need a different kind of competence. I haven't lost my strength, it's just that I need to reconfigure what it looks like, how I express it, because my circumstances have changed. I need to concentrate on the agency that remains, experiment with using it, and keep on keepin' on, like an Energizer bunny. Make the container bigger, the view larger and longer . . .*

Thus, I worked to avoid mistaking post-loss disorientation for personal invalidation, reminding myself that it takes time to grow into new definitions, new circumstances.

Writer Christina Baldwin offers a hopeful idea to foster this transition: "When you're stuck in a spiral, to change all aspects of the spin, you only need change one thing." If I can practice being definitive in small ways, gradually I'll find my way back to my true rhythm.

When you doubt your power,
you give power to your doubt.

~ *Honoré de Balzac*

EYES OF WONDER

GRACE HAD led me safe thus far, although at the time I could not yet have named the power that was getting me from one day to the next. I had not yet identified what was holding me. Being able to name and inhabit that presence was step one, a gift from Grace itself.

Despite identifying this ineffable gift, I was still weary, bone-weary. My bag of tricks was empty. I needed another talisman, a partner to work in tandem with Grace.

Although it can be many things, the Grace most present for me in those hard months was largely inner-directed, comforting, holding, and shielding me from things I could not yet handle. Inside my self-imposed cocoon, however, a nascent voice was badgering me to break open and find ways to embrace the world beyond myself. I needed a different muse, one that could inspire me to action, a guiding light to show me new ways to proceed.

The missing piece popped into view. No doubt it was there all along but became evident only when I was ready to see it: Curiosity.

* * *

Notes from my journal tell the story. Eleven months into my journey, the entries spewed vague messages that prompted me to see my counselor. Following my session with her, I continued the conversation in my journal:

Okay... So I'm lonely. Embrace it. If that's how I feel, do it well. ("Feel what you feel," remember that?) Celebrate the "good" parts... (More about that later.)

If lonesome takes over, do something about it! Call someone. Go somewhere. Make an active choice.

Think of new alternatives.

*Develop eyes of wonder... Instead of bracing myself against an onslaught of negativity, **have eyes of wonder.** The very term is full of promise.*

What does it mean?

- *Basic, childlike faith in the all-rightness of things*
- *Childlike acceptance of what comes my way*
- *Zest*
- *Reverence for life*
- *Compassion*
- *Curiosity*

Curiosity! Curiosity offers a new vantage point. It leaves behind judgments and recriminations by replacing them with questions.

- What's going on here?
- Is there a message in what is happening?

- What have I failed to notice?
- What possibilities are hiding in plain sight?
- How can I view things differently?
- What if I turned away from those closed doors and looked for cracked-open windows?
- How am I allowing my past to define my present?
- Help is always at hand if one is open to it and looks for it. Where is help, right in this very moment?

The list of possible questions seems endless.

Poet/philosopher David Whyte calls these "beautiful questions." In his seminars and writings, he encourages digging deep to find and then articulate the vague uncertainties that plague us so we can frame them into questions to grapple with them. He goes on to suggest that these discerning questions will yield revelations from unexpected quarters, with possibilities showing up in surprising ways and places—strong encouragement to keep our radars sharply tuned lest we miss opportunities.

Questions are Curiosity made manifest. They unleash new energy and the possibility to notice Grace, which is always waiting nearby.

My mantra became, *What would eyes of wonder see?* Eyes of wonder stretched my curiosity to see beyond perceived boundaries and assumptions. They ask open, deeper, unschooled, even outrageous questions, faithful that the process itself will show the way forward.

Ready, set, go!

SMALL PLEASURES

In spite of illness, in spite even of the
arch-enemy sorrow, one can remain alive
long past the usual date of disintegration
if one is unafraid of change, insatiable
in intellectual curiosity, interested in
big things, and happy in small ways.

~ *Edith Wharton*

ACTIVELY NURTURING a positive outlook, even
when weighed down by great sadness or upheaval, is
perhaps the single most healing thing we can do for
ourselves in pursuit of greater overall well-being.

Research shows that body chemistry and mental
abilities are influenced by mindset. Neural pathways
alter as they accommodate input and "decide" how
to track, judge, and store incoming information.
Default circuitries develop according to which
thoughts we reinforce. These change as we alter our
thought patterns, a process called neuroplasticity.

The brain is a complex, fine-tuned machine, evolved
over eons to handle everything from breathing
without thinking to high-order decision-making.

Part of the way it manages all these tasks is by developing shortcuts based on experience, making it more efficient and able to handle more (and more complex) issues. Once established, these pathways act largely on autopilot. (If x, then y . . .)

When mired in grief, shock, and fear, it's easy to go down rabbit holes of awfulizing, seeing only negative possibilities. Unwittingly, this reinforces the very things we seek to dispel, meaning that as the brain assesses each ensuing moment, attention will default to the scary, unsettled, darker possibilities of the moment.

It's a mental merry-go-round wherein momentum begets momentum—in this case, in an unwelcome, unhelpful direction. Developing (or remembering) a positive attitude to reverse energy direction requires deliberate intention and steadfast commitment. It's not a simple, once-and-done exercise. It requires constant reinforcement.

It helps to remember that we do not "betray grief by feeling joy. You are not being graded, and you do not receive extra credit for being miserable 100% of the time," writes author Maggie Smith. "Find pockets of relief, even happiness, when and where you can. Keep moving."

The first order of business is to stop negative momentum. Nothing good can happen until adverse motion is stopped. In one of her essays, writer Cheryl Strayed says that the way to stop is to stop! "It really is that easy." Although she's writing about jealousy, her words bear wider application: you stop by shutting down counterproductive messages, replacing them with an idea that will help you. Fake it 'til you make it . . .

The next challenge is creating energy to move in a positive direction, however slightly, however tentatively. Like *The Little Engine That Could*, gathering strength and speed with each repetition of "I think I can . . . I think I can . . . I think I can . . ."

How can I unlock this energy? Once more, Curiosity is my ally here.

Curious and open, I intentionally coax myself to look for small pleasures. Instead of focusing on looming problems, I concentrate on nurturing gratitude and possibility wherever I see it. My brain will respond by rewiring neural pathways to accommodate these altered viewpoints. Ideas that soothe and delight will rise to the top of my consciousness while those that frighten and disturb will start to fade into the background. It's all about where I put my intention and energy. When I alter the flow of incoming information, the response will alter as well. As the Italian proverb says, "For a web begun, God sends a thread."

Once the merry-go-round gains momentum in this new direction, possibilities and pleasures pop up all over the landscape. Suddenly there is color where none existed before. Visions of potential and promise emerge from barren vistas.

Often unremarkable in isolation, little delights add up and make difficult slogs like grieving more bearable, such as:

- Noticing the first daffodils of spring.
- The comfort of sitting by the fire.
- Walking in nature, in forests or woods, by lakes or oceans. Or right in my neighborhood, breathing fresh air, noticing what's going on.
- Reading a "guilty pleasure" novel without feeling the need that everything must have a high-minded purpose.
- Making a pot of soup and savoring the delectable aromas as they fill my home.
- Staying in pj's all day on a rainy day.
- Indulging in little expressions of self-care, like scented candles or really good hand lotion.

This can be a truly lovely merry-go-round! Positive thoughts reveal positive prospects that renew my confidence and energize new initiatives. (I could go on . . .)

It surprised me (although it should not have) that, over time, as my brain relaxed, I found myself daring bigger pleasures:

- Travel, even solo travel.
- Replacing two chairs in my living room as a tangible investment in the future, turning away from "the best is behind me" thinking.
- Reclaiming my voice! Healthy enough, finally, to stop hiding, playing it safe, and risk being fully real instead of "selectively" so. (More about this in Chapter Five.)

It all started with cultivating small pleasures, each one leading to the next. Another series of breadcrumbs . . .

CHAMBERED NAUTILUS

MY PATH forward was not as clear-cut as these anecdotes may imply. At times the essays may read like lesson plans, but there was no instruction book for me to follow. It was never as simple as "Do *x* and you'll feel better." I improvised, listened to my spirit, tried what occurred to me, and trusted that somehow, at some point, the fog would lift, and I'd find my way.

Much of my journey is better described as two steps forward, one (or two or three) steps back. Not to mention detours, side trips, and various trial-and-error experiments. The point is that I stayed in the game. I refused to remain on the bench. I got out on the field. Sometimes I fouled out. Sometimes I ran too fast, sometimes I fell down, but I always got back up. Occasionally, I scored a point. Regardless, *I stayed in the game.* You can't move forward if you wait on the sidelines.

Bouncing around, though—there's the pendulum again—I needed another steadying idea to rally around.

It came from Mark Nepo in *The Book of Awakening: Having the Life You Want by Being Present to the Life*

You Have. In one of his meditations, he ponders how "we resolve and integrate where we've been before."

> A great model for us exists in the chambered nautilus... Over time it builds a spiral shell, but always lives in the newest chamber and uses the others to stay afloat. Can we, in this way, build strong chambers for our traumas: not living there, but breaking our past down till it is fluid enough to lose most of its weight?

Nepo suggests that we allow painful memories a deliberate place in our spirits as well as a role in our lives. Instead of expunging these memories, we would be better served by sealing them lovingly in various corners of our hearts, honoring their lessons and their role in making us who we are. Using the past as leaven instead of being weighed down by it adds buoyancy to our lives and helps keep us afloat.

The power of this image completely inspired me. I bought a lovely print of a chambered nautilus, framed it, and hung it where I would see it every day. Nepo's analogy reenergizes me every time I see this print. Another speck of light on my horizon...

CHAPTER FOUR

AMBUSHED BY VOLCANIC ANGER

Anger is loaded with information and energy.

~ *Audre Lord*

FURY BREAKS THROUGH
SELF-DELUSION

Of all the people on the planet, you talk to
yourself more than anyone.
Make sure you are saying the right things.

~ Author unknown

AND YET. All those breadcrumbs, all those
helpful insights could not stave off the inevitable
eruption of Vesuvius spewing forth venom and
anger. ANGER! Not your everyday garden variety of
annoyance but blind rage.

From my journal:

*Furioso: In a tempestuous and vigorous manner.
Used chiefly as a direction.*

*All righty, then. It seems I have neglected to notice
that this Sonata Form a la Grief has a required
movement: A-N-G-E-R., anger. You know, the kind
we civilized, enlightened, wise, Buddha-aspiring
people do not allow ourselves.*

*Well, I'm here to tell you that ten months, seven days,
one Thanksgiving, one Christmas, one Mother's Day,
two birthdays, one Father's Day, and one child's*

wedding later, I am finally discovering the depths of ANGER. I am sick to death of being long-suffering and sad, of trying to put one foot in front of the other, of being @#$%^&* positive.

My clue is the emerging use of foul language, language I am not accustomed to using. Out loud. (How convenient! I live alone! No one to be shocked and outraged!)

Here's the problem, though. I don't know where to put my anger, at whom to direct it. I want to organize it, latch it on to some "acceptable" scapegoat. God? Can't go there... God has God's reasons; I truly believe that. God will take care of me, too, I know that. Jack? How unfair! He's dead, for crying out loud. He hardly wanted to die—not "fair" to be angry with him. What or whom does that leave me?

Well, for one thing, all these people who tell me how bright the future is, how I am turning a page on the past, how I should "move on," how I need to look ahead, not back. WHAT DO THEY KNOW? Have they slept alone for ten months? Have they had to deal with all the vicissitudes, the quandaries, the broken clerestory windows, the tax forms, the mail that comes to the deceased? @#$$%^& looking ahead... the past seems far more attractive.

It's as if there is this caged beast—a roaring tiger, I'm thinking—being sent to me as part of the grief package. ("Here: Deal with this if you can!") Here's the catch: two phrases in small print at the bottom of the accompanying instruction sheet say: "Not Optional" and "Must Be Released—Outcome Unknown."

Well, today, I officially open the door of that cage. I don't even care where it leads. I can no longer deal with things as they are. I need a new ingredient, something to mix things up, move me along.

I'm considering breaking every dish I own. I know, I know ... that seems a bit extreme, and after all, there are people who don't have plates, people who need them. See—"civilized" is getting in my way again ...

Sigh ... what to do, what to do. I tried removing my wedding ring. I have not had it off (except for resizing) in thirty-seven years, eleven months, and one week. It feels like heresy to take it off, but I remind myself that I can put it back on. I can no longer be married to a man who does not live on the same plane that I do. I took off the ring at least an hour ago, and there is no sign of the indentation mark going away. How appropriate. Your mark on me will never end, nor do I want it to. In fact, my hunch is that one of the things that impedes the grief process is the irrational fear that memories and marks of the deceased will disappear. What I want is the happy memories, not fears, a bright outlook, confidence in the future, and not loneliness. Is that asking too much????? "'Til death us do part ..." Oh my dearest, sweet Jack. I will love you forever, but I must get on, somehow, with living here on earth ...

* * *

Ambushed by Volcanic Anger

I remember the moment with stunning clarity. I was standing in my living room, looking out over the wooded ravine below when a bellow from deep within my soul burst forth. Howls of anguish encapsulated in sobs and shouts of the absolute worst, most impolite, X-rated language in my lexicon. My little corgi, Daisy, froze in place, looking at me with eyes that said, *Who is this? What just happened? How can I get away?*

It was alarming to feel so out of control but also oddly fascinating. I intuitively sensed that something important was happening. Some needed sea change was underway. Huh!

Lurking at the edge of my consciousness was a truth I was loathe to face: dealing with anger was an unresolved issue for me. My pattern was avoidance, and what we avoid keeps knocking at our door, perhaps politely at first, but then louder and with more force until we pay attention. My outburst was my inner anger saying, *Listen to me! Deal with me! I have lessons for you, lessons you need if you are going to get beyond this abyss.*

* * *

To get a grip I needed to step back and consider my overall relationship with anger. Not just when under duress of grief, but over my entire life up to that point.

I was a tender-hearted child with a strong need for harmony, so my earliest memory of anger is of being afraid of it. Not consciously, more like a cloud of insecurity looming over my sense of well-being. In my limited experience, the results of anger were negative, threatening, and destabilizing.

I saw no positive or productive aspects to it. When anger showed up, whether in me or in those around me, the result was loss of control, and as a child, I already had very little of that. I needed to keep what I had in place to protect myself.

Coupled with that, during my early formative years a clear moral imperative took hold. The messages were varied—some subtle, some pointedly blunt— but they all emphasized the same point: expressing anger is uncivilized, and "good people" must, above all, be civil. Anger came to be equated with a lack of breeding.

I know, I know. That is convoluted, flawed thinking, but children have limited ability to evaluate the wisdom of their thoughts. My default response was a combination of avoidance, accommodation, and manipulation. Pathetic soup, that, but it generally got me where I needed to go in one piece. Until it didn't. Until deep grief overtook my life. The barren landscape of that situation revealed no detour signs labeled "This Way to Avoidance" or "This

Way to Accommodation." A potential side road to "Manipulate Things?" Nowhere to be seen.

YOU GET TO CHOOSE

Anger is a bear, but if you pay attention,
you'll hear it roaring useful instructions
about how you should steer your future.

~ *Martha Beck*

IN OVER my head, I made an appointment with
my counselor.

An essential concept crystallized as we talked,
offering me some breathing room. I could *use* anger
to *defuse* it. "Anger is energy," said my counselor. "It's
not bad in and of itself. It's what you DO with it that
matters. You de-energize it by acknowledging it and
channeling it." Unacknowledged, anger turns on
itself, turns inward. It becomes self-blame ("I should
be better than this") and/or amorphous depression,
sinking below the level where objective thought and
actions are possible.

Unacknowledged, anger grows like mushrooms in
dimly lit dung piles. Cast in the light of day, those
mushrooms shrivel.

I can be angry without lashing out, blaming
others, and creating havoc—behaviors that are

not only unproductive but also unsatisfying. I can acknowledge dark emotions but also modify self-talk, replacing messages of recrimination and self-flagellation with invitations to befriend myself with tenderness and compassion. "This is hard. I'm overwhelmed" is an objective assessment, not a "poor me pity party." It's not good or bad; it's authentic, and being authentic is the only effective, enduring road to resolution.

Anger and despair do not magically dissipate but admitting to myself that I needed comfort started the process, lowering the ante, somehow. Sometimes I avoided acknowledging this out of fear that no friend would be available when I needed one. This is realistic. People, even people who care very much about me, are busy with their own lives.

There is, however, one friend who *always* has time for me, my friend within: the core essence, the full manifestation of the person I was created to be. Over time I had lost my sense of connection to her presence and her wisdom. The vicissitudes of life had slowly, insidiously obscured her.

The road to healing required restoring an intimate reconnection with her, rediscovering her in all her rich and varied fullness. Inhabiting her, I could give full, uncensored voice to the entire range of my emotions. I could begin to remember how to extend to myself the kindness I readily offer to others.

This was a powerful place to start as I sought to dissipate my despair and anger. Okay, so I'm angry. That's an irrefutable part of the sum total of who I am. There, I've admitted it. So what? Now what?

My anger, as it turns out, was largely a *secondary* issue.

My morning readings led the way to fitting pieces together, pointing to the central role that fear plays in *everything*. Brené Brown addresses the intricate interrelationships of human emotions in *Atlas of the Heart: Mapping Meaningful Connection and the Language of Human Experience.* There's a chapter provocatively entitled "Places We Go When We Feel Wronged: Anger, Contempt, Disgust, Dehumanization, Hate, Self-Righteousness." (Yikes: an ugly stew, yet all these feelings are undeniably part of being human, so this is a "stew" to be reckoned with.)

Brown's assessments lead to an intriguing, helpful idea: "... anger [often] is a secondary or 'indicator' emotion..." The catchall feeling I'd labeled "anger" may well have been a foil for other things like fear, shame, helplessness, humiliation, isolation, depression, loneliness, or a myriad of other emotions. Whether directly or obliquely, consciously or unconsciously—anytime we're struggling, most likely it is fear in one of its many disguises that has us by the shorthairs, twisting our judgment and ability to think clearly.

Reviewing the path of my Planet Widow journey, I realize that denial of anger was a necessary, albeit unconscious, initial coping strategy. Unfortunately, the veneer that covered the dark side also hid the light.

To move beyond that façade, three things had to coalesce: acknowledge the anger, give it voice, and learn to see that it is generally intertwined with, even caused by, fear. It wasn't only anger I needed to deal with; it was the fears that lay underneath it. I had failed to make that crucial connection.

Rebirth required this integration, but it could only happen in its own good time, when I was healed enough to grapple with the magnitude and implications of this interrelationship.

My questions changed. Instead of focusing on surface appearances—in this case, anger—I looked for possible underlying causes. Instead of asking, "What do I do with this? How can I discharge it?" I asked, "What is *behind* this? What is making me feel this way?" Then asking, "What *other* feelings and emotions are also at work here?"

Although anger was shouting the loudest, my real issue was fear. I was afraid. Afraid of loneliness, of managing by myself, of feeling inadequate. Afraid of just about everything, fueled by feeling a total loss of control.

The all-encompassing mask of anger obscured and blended these challenges and issues. These are far more approachable when broken down into bite-size, discrete pieces. Different struggles require different approaches. Unmasked, I could begin to tackle them one at a time without grinding to a stop because I was overwhelmed.

My journal entries began to take on a more compassionate tone:

> *Of course I'm angry! This was a huge loss, outside normal expectations. I don't have to have someone to blame, some place to put my feelings, to be angry. I can be angry because it's hard. Angry because I'm afraid. Angry because I'm not in control. It's okay to be angry!*

Author Cheryl Strayed lost her mother when she was a teenager. She struggled with anger for decades. She writes, "You go on by doing the best you can. You go on by being generous. You go on by being true. You go on by offering comfort to others who can't go on. You go on by allowing the unbearable days to pass and by allowing the pleasure in other days. You go on by finding a channel for your love and another for your rage."

The call to befriend myself was a reminder to let go of outgrown mindsets, get off autopilot, and turn on my radar to reveal the insights popping up around me like dandelions in springtime, sparking unexpected synchronicities and connections. Serendipities abound if we can train ourselves to notice them. They lead us to the connections we seek, but we've got to be tuned in and listening closely.

Anger is scary. But faced head on, it need not be incapacitating. Acknowledging it precedes moving beyond it. Naming fears directly creates a truce of sorts by opening alternate emotional channels, allowing slack, forbearance, a different outlook, and grace to take hold.

Possibility beckoned, bidding me to abide in the fullness of the present, to trust in the ultimate rightness of things. Nothing outward had changed, but inklings of peace began to seep into the cracks of my weary heart.

Inner reconciliation began.

CHAPTER FIVE

MORE
BREADCRUMBS

Trust Future You to handle some of what
Present You is grappling with.

Future You will know more and hurt less.

~ Maggie Smith

FROM FEAR TO COMPASSION

To fear is one thing. To let fear grab you by
the tail and swing you around is another.

~ Katherine Paterson

QUANTUM LEAP forward: I began recognizing
how much fear was controlling my life. Never mind
"breadcrumbs," this was a chunk of muffin, right in
front of my eyes.

Fear skews objectivity because it attaches meaning
to facts. "She didn't call" might become "She didn't
call because she doesn't care about me." Objectively
speaking, I don't *know* why she didn't call. All I know
is that she didn't.

In its extreme, "I'm lonely" can become "No one
wants to be with me." Objectively, it means only
that I'm feeling alone, but feeling a connection with
others is such a primal need sewn into our DNA
that it's next to impossible to stick to that single fact
without inferring deeper meaning.

Attaching meanings to facts—no matter how
ensconced in primal needs those may be—impedes

my ability to think clearly. It distorts my judgment and inhibits constructive assessment and actions. Before my active imagination leads me further astray, I should determine "What are the facts? What is undeniably, objectively true in this moment, without any add-ons?"

If I'm going to attach meaning to "lonely," it would be beneficial to avoid leaping to judgments about the role others play in that situation and stick to my own part in the equation. This requires reframing the inner messages that have been weighing me down, and the ability to do that starts with compassion.

Just what is compassion, anyway? Merriam-Webster defines it as "sympathetic consciousness of others' distress together with a desire to alleviate it." The crux here is the word "other." I need to include myself on my recipient list of "others." When I do, fear's grip starts to loosen.

Self-compassion means replacing a steady diet of recriminations with messages of consolation and hope. It's about *kindness*, about pledging to treat myself with at least as much gentle consideration as I routinely extend to others, even others I don't especially like.

This shift in mindset requires keen discipline to prevent backsliding into the default messages of fear that I have reinforced so thoroughly over time. It demands intention and attention.

Self-compassion creates breathing room to relax and evolve. It sure feels better! Encouragement, even self-generated encouragement, soothes my spirit. It offers a sense of reprieve. Acknowledging the reality of my painful feelings objectively, without adding judgments, helps dissolve toxic thought patterns.

A welcome truce, indeed.

STOP STARING AT
CLOSED DOORS

It all begins with knowing nothing lasts forever,
so you might as well start packing now.

In the meantime,
practice being alive . . .

There is a you telling you another story of you.
Listen to her . . .

You belong.
Here.

~ Pádraig Ó Tuama
How to ~~Belong~~ Be Alone[*]

FACT: NO amount of staring at a permanently
closed door will reopen it.

And yet . . . when that door concealed the life I had
known for a long time, it was hard to look anywhere
else. Impossible to think realistically. To *accept* that
that door will never open again.

Joan Didion describes this poignantly in *The Year of
Magical Thinking.* "I could not give away the rest of

---

[*] From How to ~~Belong~~ Be Alone, *Feed the Beast*, Broken Sleep Books 2022.
Used with permission of the author.

his shoes. I stood there for a moment, then realized why: he would need shoes if he was to return . . ."

It's not surprising that grieving people have lapses in rational thinking. In the early throes of grief, nothing has a name, except perhaps "terror."

Life as I knew it was upended. Being without the person I'd been sharing my life with for decades felt like an extended bad dream. It was incomprehensible to me that this might be a permanent condition. Surely, I'd wake up? Best to keep that door within my line of vision, just in case . . .

I needed to fully inhabit the permanence of my situation before I could expand my sight lines. For that to happen, my spirit needed time to catch up with my new reality.

We have only a finite breadth of vision, however. Keeping that door in sight meant I had less scope to see other things. My focal point could not change until I realized what I was doing: a slow metamorphosis. As the stark reality of my situation came into sharp focus, so did the realization that it was time to look around.

My survival instincts kicked in. I learned to catch myself mid-thought. *Oh, there I go again. This isn't working. That door is closed. Expand the view. Pull out the wide-angle lens to see "other."*

It didn't always work, of course, but the chink in my armor grew, and little by little I began to explore my larger surroundings, looking for other doors and windows.

Breadcrumbs discovered one by one do not exist in isolation. They are related to one another. They interact and combine to form larger truths and expose greater possibilities. Finding small pleasures is an act of compassion. Pleasures are often found by looking beyond closed doors. Or is it that we find compassion when we stop staring at closed doors and, therefore, can notice small pleasures? It's hard to say which is a precursor to which, but when combined, the whole becomes more than the sum of the parts, the breadcrumb trail gaining definition and momentum.

LISTEN TO YOUR BODY

The body knows. When your heart sinks.
When you feel sick to your gut.
When something blossoms in your chest.
When your brain gloriously pops.
That's your body telling you the
One True Thing. Listen to it.

~ Cheryl Strayed

LIKE MANY a girl of my generation, I was brought up to be wary of my body. Anything beneath the neck was suspect. Although largely unspoken, the message was clear: don't *trust* your body, *control* it.

I get it. Young people, unable to understand how to inhabit their evolving bodies, how to be comfortable in their own skins, can be led astray easily. The price for doing so can be high, especially for girls, with the possibility of an unwanted pregnancy threatening to alter their lives indelibly. Best to be cerebral! Best to stay self-contained!

Although initially aimed at the "dangers" of sex, for me those tacit messages unconsciously morphed into mind/body disconnection. *Don't listen to tension*

or queasiness or general miasma—master your feelings!
Bury them! Control them! Have the discipline to "feel"
*what you **think** you should feel.*

It doesn't work that way, of course. We feel what we
feel. We can choose what we *do* about those feelings,
but they are what they are, independent of our
ability to fabricate them. While our minds assess our
emotions, those emotions live in the body, in our
very senses. I had no idea.

But I learned. When Jack died, I experienced feelings
not only as mental commentary but also *physically,*
in ways I was unable to control. Sitting by the fire
one Saturday morning struggling to breathe, I had
the palpable sense of a huge weight sitting on my
chest, not figuratively but literally. *I couldn't breathe,*
for heaven's sake! Already terrified and disoriented,
my body was now out of control as well? How
could I deal with a body that I could not wrestle
into submission?

It was a tenuous time. Sometimes the only way
change can come is to be driven to our knees,
desperate enough to submit to forces we don't
understand. It took a problem larger than my self-
discipline could handle to get my attention and
force a course correction. My spirit depleted, I
gave up. I prayed for courage to persevere. I asked
to be shown what I needed to learn to go on. In
desperation, I opened myself to change.

Lessons emerged from my training as a life coach. I learned that emotions live not in the brain but on a cellular level in the body. Feelings are *feelings,* not *thinkings!* Our bodies are our *friends*, not adversaries to be subdued and conquered. Bodies have innate, intuitive wisdom, but we must discover how to hear their messages. I had to learn a new language, learn to understand songs without words.

Ironically, reconnecting my mind and body became possible by considering the body as its own separate entity. I spoke to it directly: *Body, what are you telling me?*

Hearing its answers was deceivingly simple but challenging to put into practice, requiring absolute quiet. Once still enough, it becomes possible to fathom what the body is saying by doing a body check for *feelings—Are my shoulders tight? Does my throat constrict—*instead of a mind scan for *thoughts* about those sensations like *I'm sad* or *I'm frightened.*

No judgments allowed. Just assessment, followed by breathing into the feelings, allowing them recognition so they can ride on through. That's the crux: allowing the *motion* part of emotion. Otherwise we're stuck; we're at the mercy of a body doing its own thing while we cluelessly try to cut it off at the pass.

Allowing my body equal voice, my braced perspective dissolves with a profound sigh of relief: *Oh. That's what I'm feeling. Yes, yes … it's uncomfortable, but it's a messenger. A messenger! What is this sensation telling me? What could the larger message be?*

A larger message may or may not appear. It may or may not be clear. Things may or may not change outwardly. What *does* change is the locus of my perception, and that is a huge part of getting unstuck. New solutions generally evolve from new perspectives.

So, body, I thank you for your sturdy presence. I'm grateful that you show up for the job day after day, silently supporting me even when I ignore you. "We" do better when we interrelate and let each part of "us" do the job it does best. You have razor-sharp detection skills, tuned in to the real me, impervious to extraneous prattle. I need my thoughts as well, but I have given them outsized importance, allowing them to blur your wisdom. Better to let my mind play to its strengths, which are analysis and constructing supporting strategies. Better a duet than dueling solos.

Be strong then, and enter into your own body;

There you have a solid place for your feet.

Just throw away all thoughts
of imaginary things, and stand
firm in that which you are.

~ Kabir

WARMER, COLDER

When your heart speaks, take good notes.

~ Renée Locks

WHEN AND how to move forward and make decisions? Pay attention to your inclinations instead of "shoulds."

This breadcrumb came from life coach training with Martha Beck. She suggests that we use the lens of the children's game of "warmer or colder" as a decision-making tool. Remember that game? It entailed wandering around a room where someone had picked out something, the task being to figure out what that was. The only clues were being told whether you were warmer or colder (closer or farther) from the chosen object. Beck proposes that this simple measure—warmer or colder—is often an effective way to decide what to do. Does it feel warmer, as in promising—is something pulling you in? Or does it feel colder, as in arduous, unwanted, repellant, perhaps even painful? As my son says, "If it's not a 'hell yes,' it's a no!"

We can't make all our decisions based on what feels good, but we generally have far more agency than we think we do. If I don't have to do something I don't want to do, I shouldn't do it! Period. Doing things because I think they will please someone else is not a good reason. Never mind public opinion, all that "should" stuff. Following my spirit is the path of integrity, integrity meaning "quality or condition of being whole or undivided; completeness." When I feel whole, I feel better, and that's true even within the quagmire of loss. Inauthentic choices are exhausting, discouraging, and disheartening.

The world takes on a different aura when I look through the lens of attraction. Decision-making is easier when I flow with the energies that surround me; when I'm open, curious, willing to be uncertain, and ready to consider options from a position of their innate appeal instead of my unconsidered default positions.

The universe stands ready to help, but I must be flexible enough to let it. As Alan Cohen, teacher, coach, and author, says, "You don't have to make anything happen. Just align yourself with what wants to happen and let it." Stop overthinking, overplanning, and trust that things will work out as they should.

Sometimes I just need to get out of my own way.

When faced with a decision, I ask myself what is truly required. Do I have agency? Do I have a choice in this situation? If so, I continue with a warmer/colder assessment. What attracts me?

I go toward the sun, toward warmer. It rarely leads me astray.

CAVEAT: BALANCE IS IMPORTANT!

THE WARMER/COLDER decision-making tool is a means of being true to oneself, not license to be obsessively self-preoccupied and self-indulgent at the expense of others. The goal is to handle things in a way that is congruent with our inner natures without bypassing basic consideration of others.

It's necessary—especially early in grief—that we focus on ourselves to figure out how to "do new." It's a time of tremendous confusion. There is a limit to how many adaptations can be worked on simultaneously. Self-preservation kicks in, as well it should. We won't have anything to offer anyone else until we find a modicum of equilibrium to keep ourselves afloat.

As the days go on, however, as we get stronger, it is important to widen our view and become more aware of others. We are not the only persons who need attention, the only ones experiencing grief, deep sadness, challenges, or problems.

A balancing act is required. We need to pay attention to our own needs but also to reach out to others. Magically, doing for others alleviates our sense of isolation and loneliness in a way that concentrating on ourselves cannot.

There is another factor as well: people are busy with their own lives. Although they sympathize with the upheaval we're experiencing because of our loss, they have other things to think about. Especially if they've never experienced great loss themselves, our situations can easily fade into the background. This is not judgment or criticism but human nature. Staying on others' radar screens requires being interested in *their* situations as well as in our own.

There comes a point when it's time to "Get over yourself!"

Not as in denying our situations, but as in widening our scopes to see others' situations. Yes, sadness continues. Yes, there are challenging hurdles everywhere you look. And, yes, others have needs, too, and there is much we can do to help. Sadness tends to sharpen listening skills, make us better able to empathize deeply with others' heartaches. Widening our scopes further, there are people to befriend, community needs to be addressed, nature to be experienced, joys to be found. It's not either-or, it's both-and.

The pendulum swings back and forth as we alternately focus on our needs and stay aware of the needs of others. That's how the world works.

Our job is to avoid overly lopsided emphasis on ourselves and keep swinging until we find our place of equilibrium, a healthy balance of attention to ourselves as well as to others.

BOTH-AND

Multiple seemingly contradictory
things can be true at the same time.

IN THE early stages of grief and loss, there was only despair and sadness. As time wore on, however, I experienced wildly conflicting feelings at the same time. Moments of relative contentment crept in alongside my sorrow. It was disconcerting: How could I be content when I was also sad?

"The western mind," says Brad Stulberg, co-author of *The Growth Equation*, "is highly trained in rational, dualistic thinking, a lineage that traces itself all the way back to the ancient Greeks. Dualistic thinking is about comparison, differentiation, and splitting apart; in essence, it views the world as either this or that."

We're schooled from early childhood on to see things as either-or, starting with good or bad: it's good to share your toys but bad to keep them just for yourself. "This or that" thinking proliferates as we grow up, as we need to decide what we'll do, where we'll live, who we'll spend time with, and how we view politics. Either-or thinking—often an unconscious process—is a convenient shorthand for making decisions in a fast-paced, frenetic society.

Until it doesn't work. Until our feelings, opinions, and experiences no longer fit into convenient, tidy containers but spill over and cross-pollinate, leaving us with needing a different way to make sense of things.

Stulberg goes on: "Some things in life truly are either-or, but many are both-and. Ancient wisdom traditions such as Buddhism and Taoism understand and teach the paradoxical nature of reality. They develop a non-dual mind." They encourage us to see a bigger picture wherein we can incorporate seeming opposites into a larger whole. Thus:

- We need to work hard *and* to rest.
- Self-discipline *and* self-compassion are both necessary, the former hard to sustain without the latter.
- We need solitude *and* community. The proportions of these need to change with our circumstances, so we need to be ever mindful of balancing them, not ruling out one in favor of the other.

Accordingly, happiness *and* sadness can also coexist. Our human hearts are large enough to hold both concurrently.

Being reminded that contradictory emotions can coexist was key to loosening the logjam of disparate thoughts that had me in a stranglehold. *This reminder offered me permission to be happy while also honoring deep sadness.* I didn't have to choose one or the other. My weary heart could hold it all. Indeed, holding it all is the path to transformation, allowing inklings of contentment to soothe the sharp edges of sorrow. Great sadness *and* small pleasures. Grief *and* joy.

Clinging to "either-or" thinking stunted my forward motion. It kept me so busy trying to decide what I was feeling that I became stuck in rigid definitions, unable to allow the messiness of growth or the grace of inklings, not to mention precluding any sense of respite. Either-or goads and challenges. Both-and offers breathing room with an invitation to see things differently.

Author and educator Parker Palmer writes about this in *A Hidden Wholeness: The Journey Toward an Undivided Life.* He counsels us to learn to

> *hold the tension of opposites, trusting that the tension itself will pull our hearts and minds open to a third way of thinking and acting . . . . Uncomfortable*

> *with holding the tension of conflicting viewpoints
> and wanting to 'get on with it,' we call the question,
> take the vote, and let the majority decide what course
> we should take.... But by cutting the exploration
> short, we have deprived ourselves of a chance to find
> a better way by allowing opposing ideas to enrich
> and enlarge each other until a new vision emerges.*

To access the "new," something must intrude upon the "old." Fighting the process only lengthens and exaggerates it. Permission—indeed, encouragement—to widen my lens and embrace contradictory feelings or opinions leads to new understandings and ways of being.

Living is a dynamic, unfolding, and surprising experience, often fraught with doubts and hurdles. We don't get to choose what comes our way, but we do get to decide how to respond. When conflicting ideas emerge, emerging into wholeness begins with making the container large enough for both-and instead of locking ourselves in straitjackets of either-or.

REVISITING THE
TRAPEZE

I'VE ALWAYS loved trapezes! When I was a child, a trapeze hung from a high catalpa branch in our backyard. I remember contorting myself up and over the bar, swinging with abandon, free and joyous.

At the circus, my favorite thing was watching aerial artists. I held my breath as they let go of one trapeze, flying with abandon toward another headed their way. Yes, there was a safety net, but empty air in between still seemed mighty scary. The trick is timing, of course, but there is another significant element: *You have to let go of one bar in order to grab the other.*

Or not: in my mind's eye, I see what would happen if the artist lacked the faith to let go. There she is, hanging from two trapezes, one arm clenching the initial bar, the other gripping the oncoming one. She stops in midair because motion cannot continue until she lets go of one bar or the other.

That lesson applies to finding new ways of putting a life together, as well.

Clergyman and peace activist William Sloane Coffin once observed that when a loved one dies it's not so much they we have lost—what are really lost are our expectations.

"Expectations" are like that first trapeze bar. If I cling to them, I can't begin to grasp alternatives. What was is behind me now. The question is whether I will dare to let go and reach for what is headed my way.

Leaps should be chosen with intention after objective observation. Openness does not mean indiscriminate, willy-nilly grasping at every passing opportunity. But there comes a point when I can no longer hold on to two things at once, when the choice is to leap with faith or to stagnate. There's always that safety net if my timing is off or the oncoming bar is a mirage.

Better to leap than to wither in frozen immobility.

"NOT HELPFUL!"

EARLY IN widowhood I found it difficult and challenging to set boundaries. Well-meaning friends had so many ideas about what I should do, where I should live, how I should spend my time, etc.

I hesitated to offend people by debating with them. I could not afford to lose anyone else in my life because I felt so completely and desperately alone. Besides, I was completely unmoored. I didn't know what to do or what to think, making it difficult to have meaningful conversations.

Overwhelmed, I tended to shut down, not so much "passive" as "not present." I'm sure that stance—an unusual one for me—alarmed those who loved me.

People who love us often have a hard time simply standing by and witnessing our grief. Until they have experienced deep grief themselves, they often don't realize that the greatest gift they can offer bereaved friends is that of witness, of listening, of standing alongside. Bereaved people need to be heard and held, not problem-solved. My friends wanted to make me feel better, so they suggested "solutions."

I didn't need their solutions. I needed their presence.

Catch-22: I needed to assert myself before I even knew who that self was!

How could I do that?

I decided I needed a well-rehearsed stock phrase that I could pull out when I didn't know how else to respond. I came up with *I appreciate your concern, but these ideas are not helpful right now.* Although it took courage to say it the first time, I was pleasantly surprised then and many times thereafter with the caring responses; people backed off respectfully, deferentially. Probably I could have left it at that, but I always tried to follow up with some positive comment to encourage them to stay engaged without overpowering me. I needed them; I just didn't need their opinions. I learned to set boundaries.

Boundaries are about voice, about claiming our stake in whatever is at hand. I didn't need to shout. I didn't need to be belligerent, argumentative, or judgmental. I just needed to speak my truth as I saw it, quietly, firmly, without excuse or explanation.

Although I started setting boundaries out of overwhelmed necessity, setting limits had an unexpected consequence: it was empowering. It helped me find my solo voice. It renewed my ability to be decisive, adding a glimmer of retaking control of my life.

I didn't have to know the answers to stand firm on my own two feet. All I had to do was claim my territory!

ALLOW UNFOLDING

Sometimes you don't have to figure out what
to do, you just have to allow it to happen.

~ *Ned Suesse*

RETAKE CONTROL . . . *establish boundaries* . . . Well, sorta. Give it a go. Be decisive, but keep your radar tuned in to ongoing input, because control, it turns out, is a slippery lizard. Just when you think you've got it in hand, it squirms away. What to do?

Too often, my downfall has been hanging on to an idea, an opinion, or a plan despite contrary evidence from the Universe. My MO is to keep at it, which amounts to forcing a square peg into a round hole. Tenaciously. Doggedly. An exercise in masochism: painful effort, zero reward.

As they say in poker, "You gotta know when to hold 'em and know when to fold 'em." In other words, when to keep at it, when to stop or change course.

Examples of my misguided efforts are wide-ranging and painfully personal—trying to arrange a family rendezvous, assemble music groups, establish professional associations, or make travel plans being just a few. In each case, I started with a good idea but continued to push forward when clearly the pieces were not coming together. Chief White Eagle said, "When you try to do things and they will not go the way you want, leave them alone."

Timing may be a factor. In a dream, I arrived somewhere unrecognizable and could not find the key to get in. A voice spoke. "If you get somewhere and can't find the key to get in, either you're not supposed to be there, or you've come too soon." Even persistent tenacity cannot overcome situations when the stars are not aligned favorably. Stars align on their schedule, not mine.

Things *unfold.* Part of this is planning, timing, openness to new information—and a *big* part is flexibility. An even *bigger* part is listening for deep inner knowing. It's there, but it's easy to shunt aside, blinders on, plowing full steam ahead. Nonetheless, we won't get help for the track we're not supposed to be on.

Perhaps this can be much simpler. Perhaps the underlying message is to *stop trying so hard.* To *flow,* confident in our ability to adjust our sails to match prevailing winds while steering around shoals, learning to enjoy the ride instead of trying to control it fully.

LET GO

I've decided that it's important to love
the life you get and somehow learn to
let go of the life you dreamed of.

~ *Lolly Winston*

SEVERAL YEARS after Jack's death I again heard
his voice, this time as I was walking down our lane
on a spring morning. Clear as a bell, though, no
mistaking it. *You do not honor me with sadness.*

Like his first message, this was an astonishing gift.

At the time, I was still struggling to balance the
grief of losing him with finding new ways to live.
Honoring his memory and being happy felt mutually
exclusive. "Both-and" thinking simply did not seem
to apply in this context. It was too important, too
monumental, too unimaginable.

His words gave me permission to let go and begin
again. They implied that focusing on sorrow and
loss was a disservice to his memory as well as to the
legacy of our marriage.

Forward motion is so disjointed. The pieces are there, ready to be assembled, yet we often overlook the very piece we need at a given moment.

Not long before Jack died, he and I sat on a dock in the Thousand Islands region of the St. Lawrence River, looking over the water and enjoying a glass of wine together at sunset. It was an idyllic evening, causing us to reminisce about the course of our marriage. We were feeling deeply grateful for the trajectory of our lives, counting our blessings. Happy adventures. Children successfully launched. Projects tackled together. Financial security. Health. (At least we thought so . . . little did we know that within weeks one of us would be gone.) "From here on out," said Jack, "it's icing on the cake."

One of us—oddly, I don't remember who initiated the conversation—said, "You know, someday one of us will have to live without the other. We get so much strength from our partnership, the whole being so much more than the sum of the parts. How will the one who's left behind manage alone?" The other answered, "Whoever remains will have to see the sunsets for two."

"Sunsets for two." I've often thought of that in the years since then, a talisman of sorts to guide me in moments of doubt, urging me to look for joy. "The gloom of the world is but a shadow," said Fra Giovanni, a fifteenth-century friar and scholar.

"Behind it yet, within our reach, is joy. Take Joy." My job is to live as fully as I can, to find joy wherever I can, to be open to opportunities, knowing they will look different than I imagined.

I can do that, but only if I let go. Jack's job on earth ended. Mine continues. I honor him by doing the best I can with what remains. Singer-songwriter Nightbirde reminds me: "You can't wait until life isn't hard before you decide to be happy." Being happy is a choice. It becomes possible when I stop clinging to what has ended and focus instead on the beginnings quietly beckoning me forward.

Let go. Let be. Peace cannot blossom until I begin to do that.

CHAPTER SIX

ROADBLOCK: BESIEGED BY LONELINESS

The finest thing in the world is
knowing how to belong to oneself.

~ *Michel de Montaigne*

UNMOORED

It saddens me to become once
again an independent woman.

It was a deep joy to depend on
his insight and guidance.

~ Anaïs Nin

THE UNFOLDING trail of breadcrumbs helped
me carry on, but it did not dispel loneliness. Of all
the ramifications of widowhood—sorrow, grief,
altered lifestyle, legal and financial adjustments, and
changed social circumstances—loneliness was by far
the most intractable.

Loneliness confronted me around every corner.
It slept with me at night and accosted me upon
waking, beginning the cycle all over again.
Loneliness: always lurking on the sidelines, barely
held at bay, like the hydra of Greek mythology, a
multiheaded monster that could not be overcome
with a single blow.

Loneliness. A sense of utter desolation and
removal. No English word seems to capture the
depth of isolation that I felt. A German word

served me better: *Sehnsucht,* fusing yearning, longing, nostalgia, hankering, and pining into one evocative word.

Sehnsucht—a combination of sehen, meaning "to see," suchen, meaning "to search for," and Sucht, meaning "addiction"—was my constant companion, riding shotgun wherever I went. I had a "seeing addiction," looking everywhere for that which was forever taken from me.

I felt completely lost. Utterly at sea, rudderless, anchorless, captain-less. I wanted a safe haven.

From my journal:

> *I feel like I'm stepping into the darkness. I cannot shake the odd, disengaged state of my mind. Observing more than feeling. Unusual. I keep telling myself this is the road to the next place, but it feels so singularly weird. I don't know who I am, or why I am. I say that dispassionately. It's like a very long bad dream, except that it doesn't unhinge me anymore. I just don't know what matters... Don't even know how to articulate what it is that I don't know!*

In retrospect, I can see that my slate was being wiped clean, a brutal but painful necessity for evolution. At that time the emptiness was terrifying.

A later entry:

It's not getting any easier. I am nervous so much of the time . . .

It happens on a dime. All of a sudden, I feel my body change and I am almost unable to breathe.

What am I nervous about? Being alone. No, not really. It's being without a "tether." I need connection . . .

What does lonely mean to me? Too much silence. Endless quiet evenings. No one to talk to. Solitary decision-making. Crossword puzzles instead of companionship at meals. Dealing with ALL the bailiwicks solo. It means "why?" Sharing is a human need. I long to share.

It means: Unmoored. Untethered. Lonely. Extraneous. Solitary. Isolated, devolving into feeling irrelevant, unneeded, directionless, and aimless.

A glimmer emerges: loneliness is real but adding "irrelevant, unneeded, directionless, and aimless" is a form of distortion and self-flagellation. Incorrectly attaching meanings cloud the issue rather than illuminating it.

Adjusting my lens to focus on what is relevant, I settled on one word: unmoored. *No longer tied in place. Confused, insecure,* says the dictionary. Yep— that sums it up.

Now what?

Time for objectivity. Time to get out of my head and research what experts had to say. Flickers of useful insights emerged, allowing me to begin untangling the intricate web that engulfed me.

In *On My Own: The Art of Being a Woman Alone*, psychotherapist Florence Falk writes, "We need to remind ourselves—not once, but many times—that unhappiness and fear in these beginning stages of aloneness are normal and natural; indeed, they are a necessary stage of our grief journey.... In due course we will arrive at the place we need to be."

I'd never been truly alone before, having gone from my family's home to a college dorm, to sharing an apartment with a friend, to marriage. No wonder it was hard for me to imagine being alone. Who am I without others? Who am I if I am by myself? Of course I was lonely and frightened.

Falk continues, "Healing has its own rhythm and tempo—long pauses of inertia, when it feels like nothing is happening, or ever will again. We are often obliged to abide in the inertial state of 'no thing' before change can happen of its own accord."

"Though our journey as women alone begins in fear, it ends, hopefully, in renewal ... we must be willing to allow the process of discovery to occur naturally. That means we must sit with, not run from, the discomforting feelings ... [Whatever they are.] For it is a truism that as we confront our fears, by acting in spite of and through them tentatively at first, then with increasing confidence, we begin to recover the integrity of self that we so yearn for. Integrity refers to an inner wholeness, wherein a person is not divided from herself . . ."

Befriending aloneness would be challenging, take time, and require persistence.

Falk's insights gave me some places to begin, shifting my perspective from despair, self-blame, and failing to "How can I learn to do new?" since clearly, I am in a place I've never been before.

At one point in Barbara Kingsolver's *Animal Dreams,* the protagonist Codi, worrying about people she's lost and people she loves who are in danger, says, "I didn't wish to be comforted. You can't replace the people you love with other people . . . They're not like old shoes or something." [Loyd, her lover, replies:] "No. But you can trust that you're not going to run out of people to love."

That line stuck with me, a lodestar for times when my courage ebbs. The human heart is big enough to love many people. It's not a zero-sum game. No two loves will be alike. We'll always miss the uniqueness of loved ones lost, but there will always be people to love. And people to love us!

UNTETHERED

Every bit of looking you do
contributes to finding.

~ Alan Cohen

THERE'S HOW loneliness feels on the inside.
Then there are its outward consequences, the social
considerations.

Widowhood upends long-established social
patterns. Interactions with other couples must
be renegotiated now because you are single. The
changed energy field is challenging to all involved.

As a new widow I felt raw, exposed, and vulnerable. I
wasn't sure who I was without my other half. That's
a trite expression, but it accurately describes how
I felt: torn in half, cleft down the middle, limping
along on one leg.

I had no idea if I was interesting to others on my
own. I wasn't even sure I was interesting to myself.

Old wounds resurfaced. The fear of social rejection
I'd felt starting in seventh grade had gone AWOL
during my time with Jack, conveniently allowing me

to ignore it, thinking it had evaporated. He so clearly "got" me, loving me beyond reason. I bloomed with his enthusiastic affirmation. But then he died, and those affirmations died with him.

Buried wounds do not die, however. They lie dormant until the suture ruptures, then return with renewed vengeance, demanding attention. In some ways I had been living piggyback, too often depending on reflected worth instead of believing in myself.

It was an unsettling realization. It felt like yet another failure. I wasn't looking for more problems but clearly this one was intricately related to dealing with loneliness and needed to be addressed. I needed to evolve, not criticize myself.

I had no idea how to do that.

I'd run out of courage. Lost, stopped in my tracks, no path in sight. My trusted counselor reframed it for me. "I don't think courage is what you need right now. You need hope."

I didn't know where to find that, but I bumbled on, patching things together as best I could, working concurrently to face my inner insecurity.

Just when needed most, Grace came to visit in the form of a note from one of Jack's colleagues, a lovely, thoughtful man who writes to me every year on the anniversary of my husband's death. "First of all I want to make sure you know that while I am remembering Jack on these anniversaries I am also remembering YOU! . . . You are strong, thorough, caring, kind, empathic . . ."

My body shifted as I read his note. I relaxed, sighing with relief. Someone I respected saw value in *me*, reminding me that I am loved for who I am, not just for who I was lucky enough to be married to. The old rejected me sought reflected worth, hitching my identity to someone else's. Maybe I could stop doing that. Maybe! Maybe I could start looking at who I am without apology for who I am not. Work with what I've got, call a truce, and begin to truly inhabit a mindset and a heart set that "I am enough. Just as I am, I am enough."

Grace delivered hope. Hope imparted energy. My wheels began to turn once more.

Once again, though, the question was "Now what?"

Paradigms from my former life no longer fit. The only way to be less alone is to do things with others. I needed to branch out and create new relationships while also redefining old ones.

As weeks and months went on, I tried new activities, an uneven forward-and-back exercise depending on my courage level at any given time. I went to meetings and gatherings. I called barely known acquaintances to suggest outings. Although I made some progress, it was a demoralizing slog rife with awkward self-conscious moments of feeling totally out of place. I longed to *belong,* but nothing seemed to work, to "take."

What else could I do?

Enter online dating. Yeesh. At an advanced age . . . not for the faint of heart, I assure you. It felt like going to the meat market to pick out a pork chop.

And yet—it was another breadcrumb of sorts, broadening my world. I communicated with several men and met a few in person. Some experiences were pleasant, some a bit bizarre. Most were poignant, as the men I met were as lonely and clueless as I was.

Grace led the way to some clarifying experiences as I experimented with various dating sites. I learned that I was more capable than I gave myself credit for. I realized that while I labeled myself as "lonely," I was not devastatingly so. I longed for sharing but came to see that there's nothing lonelier than being with people and feeling alone, spending time with people with whom you have little in common.

"You need to get okay alone," advised a kind man who was facing the same challenges I was. He reminded me that there is a flip side to loneliness: solitude. It was a defining moment.

In order for loneliness—as real as it is—to deplete us, we must feed it.

Loneliness is not the end of anything. It is the starting point at which we are able, this time, to choose fresh ways of being alive.

~ *Joan Chittister*

TRUCE

When the pain of loneliness comes
upon you, confront it, look at it without
any thought of running away.

If you run away you will never
understand it, and it will always be
waiting for you around the corner.

~ J. Krishnamurti

SOLITUDE CAN supersede loneliness. Embracing
it will not extinguish loneliness but rather modify
its meaning and intensity. Okay-ness with being
alone can grow if gently nurtured, but the frenetic
pace and constant noise of modern society obscures
the process.

Embracing solitude requires profound self-
acceptance. John O'Donohue writes, "I think what
happens in loneliness is that we panic; we somehow
see ourselves isolated and distant from others, and
then we really feel abandoned . . . I have learned
myself painfully that you can only relate to someone
if you somehow have the courage and the need to
inhabit your own solitude."

Letting go of inculcated ideas about connectedness, I chose to be my own best friend. I addressed my soul directly. From my journal:

> *Hi, there, Spirit. I know you are there—actually **here**, already within me—my better, wiser, eternal self. I long for honest "conversation" with you instead of holding you in distant reverence. I thought I had to be "perfect" before daring such familiarity, but I've come to realize that's not how it works. You are always ready to help and support me. I need your friendship and encouragement. With your guidance, I can learn to savor solitude instead of dreading it. I can start right now by accepting and incorporating your presence and reassurance. I know it's up to "me." Let's settle in together and relax. Let's "talk."*

Maya Angelou amplifies this sense of self-befriending in an interview with Bill Moyers. "I belong to myself. I am very proud of that. I am very concerned about how I look at Maya. I like Maya very much." "Liking oneself very much" is where contentment in solitude begins.

*   *   *

In time I came to be more or less okay with how things were. I *liked* quiet. I was grateful to be able to choose what I do and when I do it. I had friends that I could call, people I could do things with. No *anchor* but lots of tethers. It was enough, at least most of the time . . .

Sometimes I wasn't exactly lonely so much as I was afraid I *would be* lonely! I braced myself for what might happen. Rehearsing, "possessed by what isn't," as Ursula Le Guin puts it. When one does that, sure enough, she continues, "compulsions, fantasies, and terrors . . . flock to fill the void."

Contentment requires staying in the present moment. It means discounting the judgments I infer from the world at large as well as the running inner commentaries that natter at me incessantly in an endless feedback loop: "It's not normal to be content by yourself." "You should like hanging out in coffee shops and wine bars. Everyone else does." Buying into messages like these wreaks havoc with hard-won equilibrium. It's important to acknowledge reality and equally important to refrain from twisting reality by adding arbitrary meanings to it.

Instead, I learned to listen for the quiet underlying voice of my spirit, unsullied by outer judgments and illusions. As Brené Brown says, "I don't need to **change** who I am, I need to **be** who I am. The truth about who I am lives in my heart."

Gradually I began to be comfortable alone, trusting my intuition about what feels right and what doesn't as I decided what to do. The need to explain myself diminished. Self-acceptance took hold, like a lighthouse shining on the horizon pointing to the possibility of peace.

Loneliness showed up as roadblocks, shutting me down, utterly stopping me. I feared it, resisted it, and fought it, ultimately descending into its grasp because there was no detour to be found.

It was a fierce teacher. A crucible. A severe trial required to reveal depths of understanding I could not have found without it. Experiencing loneliness, I learned to understand and embrace solitude. The price was great but the reward greater.

Hafiz, the fourteenth-century Persian poet, speaks across the ages:

Don't surrender your loneliness
So quickly.
Let it cut more deeply.
Let it ferment and season you
As few human
Or even divine ingredients can.

CHAPTER SEVEN

REGAINING
TRACTION

Inhale the future, exhale the past.

~ *Author unknown*

FORK IN THE ROAD

When you get to a fork in the road, take it.

~ *Yogi Berra*

WHEN I began to acknowledge and accept my whole self—the good and the not-so-good, the best of me but also the worst, the things I was sure of and also the doubts—the engulfing fog of grief began to lift, revealing my true-north path. Stripped of false foundations and glimmering with potential grounding, a way forward gently beckoned to me.

It wasn't a straight path, however. It involved intersections requiring decisions. This way or that, every choice two choices. (Choosing to do *this,* I am also choosing *not* to do *that.*)

Making sound choices requires having good information, but in the early stages of widowhood, it was difficult to distinguish facts from illusions. The suitability of various options was often unclear, leading to "what if" thinking, slowing me down as I second-guessed where each path might lead. Since one choice precluded another, making the right judgment seemed critical. The stakes felt daunting, but I came to realize that if a given attempt didn't work, usually a course correction was possible. Many decisions are adjustable and often they are made right by the way we execute them.

At least I was in good company as I wrestled with this predicament. Many have written about it. Robert Frost in his poem "The Road Not Taken." Cheryl Strayed, referring to the life not chosen as a ghost ship: "I'll never know and neither will you about the life you didn't choose. We'll only know whatever that sister life was, it was important and beautiful and not ours. It was the ghost ship that didn't carry us. There's nothing to do but salute it from the shore."

There it is again, the importance of letting things go, be it a trapeze bar, an outgrown construct, or a ghost ship. Clinging is not helpful, and indecision is incapacitating. I needed a third option. I had to get beyond indecisive procrastination and handwringing, my default response to the ill-defined and confusing options that are hallmarks of uncharted territory.

How many times we hesitate—and hesitate again—until a unique opportunity is gone. In David Mitchell's *The Thousand Autumns of Jacob de Zoet*, the protagonist looks longingly at a woman he yearns to talk to. He hesitates, and then, visited by "The Ghost of Future Regret," he speaks.

I love the idea of deciding what to do now by considering whether I will regret not having done it in the future. Once a unique opportunity has passed, it cannot be resurrected. Better to trust my gut and go for "warmer," changing course or fine-tuning along the way as necessary.

A nexus began to crystallize. Forks in the road started to feel more like opportunities and less like threats. Connections between early breadcrumbs and new insights came into focus, as with a vision test, my sight improved with each incremental adjustment of my lens.

As the saying goes, we cannot direct the wind, but we can adjust our sails.

IN EVERY LOSS
THERE IS A GAIN

Every closed chapter is the starting point
for a new story.
Whatever is ending, let it end.
That is how beautiful things begin.

~ Martha Beck

SEEING GAINS when great loss has occurred is something I had to grow into. In the early days the very thought seemed like heresy. I wanted what I had, plain and simple.

Regaining traction, however, depends on a broader outlook.

Ripple of Loss, an exercise developed by cofounder of the Creative Grief Studio, Cath Duncan, was incredibly helpful in my movement through grief. Picture a page with three empty concentric circles. (To make your own, see note following this essay.)

In the center circle, name your primary loss—in my case, my husband.

Working outward to the next circle, name secondary losses, the things you no longer have because of the primary loss. For me those were social identity, touch, the sense of having a complete family, my anchor, equilibrium, meaning, rhythm of activity, and sense of self. On the practical side, I lost the manager of various household bailiwicks including repairs and yard work, as well as firewood provider and finance partner.

In the next circle after that, list the things you are *afraid* of losing. For me: sense of security, ability to cope, family, love, respect, touch, intimacy. Murky overlaps were evident between real losses and feared possibilities, revealing how muddled thinking becomes when we are immersed in the shock of great change.

Outside the largest circle, note the blessings that remain, the things that sustain you as you work to form new ways of being. I specifically named friends, activities I could still enjoy solo, things that gladden my heart, like music or nature—putting each within a little circle of its own to form a string of "moons" around the outside of the "lost universe" I'd just described. This offered another important symbol: light shining into the darkness.

Take the exercise a step further to notice what you are *relieved* to have lost, which can be a painful, unnerving task. My loss was shocking, horrible, and heartbreaking. I was reluctant to admit to any possible upsides to that nightmare. Also, there is no structure to this part, no encircling line. You're out there beyond organization or enclosure, in the wilds of amorphous oblivion.

But okay: I stared at the paper and began to fill in ideas outside that largest circle, each thing hard to admit, even to myself. Although immersed in grief and disorientation, I could sense the symbolic power of listing what was *outside*, beyond the definitions confined by the circles.

First on my list: I was relieved that I didn't get to choose. Had my husband lived, he would have endured a slow, agonizing death. I would have lost this vibrant, larger-than-life man millimeter by millimeter. I couldn't wish him gone, but I couldn't have wished that for him, either. I could not have chosen, so I was grateful that the choice was not mine to make.

Another: The limits I had gladly assumed to make our partnership work were gone. I could now set my own schedule, my own parameters. This was a "benefit" I wasn't sure I wanted because Jack and I were a team. We played well off each other and got a lot of strength from doing so. We'd become very comfortable working within our circumstances, deciding together how we could include as many of the things each of us wanted without sacrificing our relationship.

There were other things, as well, fuzzy with a lack of definition but rich with possibility. Who did I want to be as a single person? What financial choices would I make now that I was alone? How did my altered status change my relationship with my kids? How could I fashion a solo voice? How could I craft a way of looking at elderhood by myself?

If I was willing *then* to set boundaries within a relationship, the challenge *now* was to embrace the expanding options beyond it. It didn't matter whether I wanted these alternatives or not. New choices were available, independently of consulting anyone else. What used to be joint decisions, like what to eat or what movie to watch, like whether to rearrange the living room or go to Sweden, became choices that were now mine to make by myself. That's what was real. That's what was available. I could take it or leave it.

It can be tempting to wallow in losses, but there is no joy, no hope to be found there, and absolutely nothing to be gained from that point of view.

This was a difficult exercise, but I came to greatly appreciate and value it. It gave me an objective, tangible way to see my circumstances and options, a visible chart in place of endless thought loops. It helped me to stop hiding behind clichés to break away from an attitude of suffering and victimhood; to see a bigger picture.

In time, I found ways to thrive outside the circles, ways to "do new." I learned to embrace and enjoy the kind of spontaneity that is unique to being single. (Gotta say it again: I would not have chosen this, but since I have it, I may as well enjoy it.) I got beyond the financial angst that seems to hound every new widow, no matter what her resources are, by forging a plan that felt workable and comfortable. Slowly, I got beyond the subconscious message that because I was alone, I didn't deserve to be happy. None of these things came easily, but they did emerge over time.

Poet/philosopher John O'Donohue calls this "quarried light." "When you come through a phase of pain or isolation or suffering, the light that is given to you at the end of that is a very precious light . . . . It is the lantern that will bring you through the pain."

There are lessons to be learned and possibilities to be embraced. There are gains to be found even within great losses.

Things lost push us to find what is ours to do.

~ *Parker Palmer*

RIPPLE OF LOSS
EXERCISE

USE A large piece of paper and draw three concentric circles. Small one in the center, with ample room between the two outer circles to add written notes. Some room should remain outside the largest circle. (Paper should be at least 8½" x 11", larger is even better to give you more room to play with ideas).

1. Inside first circle, name your primary loss.
2. In the next circle, name secondary losses.
3. In the third circle, name things you are afraid of losing.
4. Use the outside of the circle to explore what is beyond. Name things that remain and sustain you. Note things you gained despite devastating loss.

Using colored pens helps to make different things stand out.

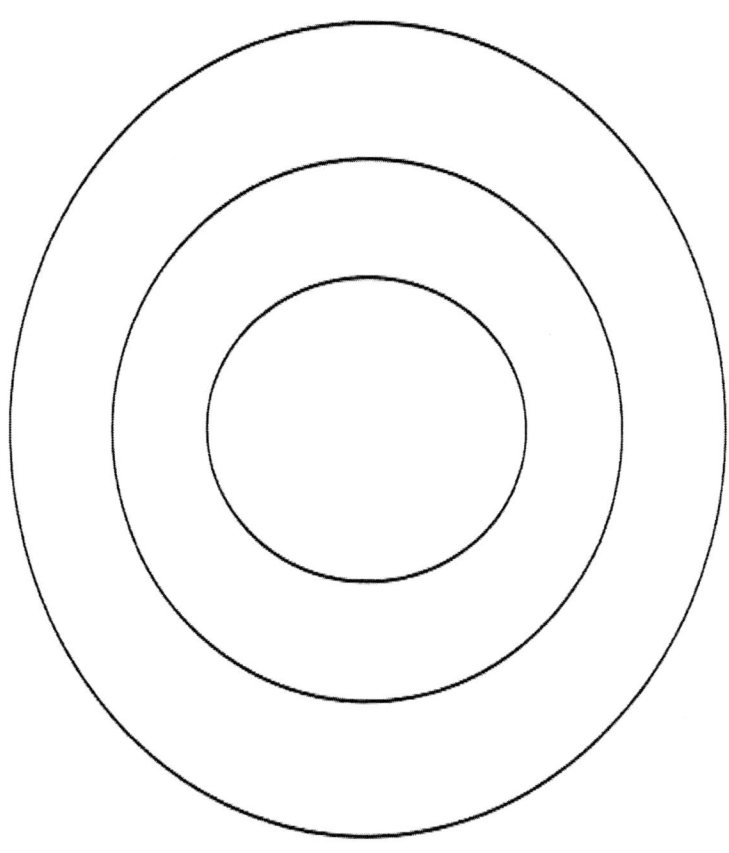

Abridged *Ripple of Loss* Exercise reprinted with permission from Cath Duncan (www.CathDuncan. com) ©2011. For a deeper dive into a guided exploration with the *Ripple of Loss*, I recommend Cath's book, *Untangle Your Grief: Questions and Art After Loss* (2021).

"YET"—"AND YET"

Have patience. Shuffle your cards.

~ Miguel de Cervantes

"YET" MEANS something that hasn't happened up until now. This little word has a big message, reminding us that things may not always remain as they are at present. Things evolve.

Maggie Smith ends her remarkable, inspiring book *Keep Moving* with this anecdote: "My daughter's third-grade teacher, Mrs. Allen, talked a lot about what she called 'the power of yet.' She'd tell the kids, 'You have not learned that . . . yet.' She'd say, 'You don't know how to do that . . . yet.'"

Any time I catch myself making a limiting statement, I repeat it, adding "yet" at the end. "I haven't figured that out . . . yet." "I don't know what to do . . . yet." "I don't have enough information . . . yet." This spawns a different sensibility. "Yet" is a word of opportunity and promise. We should use it more often.

Adding the word "and" to form "and yet" further expands the power of this word, prompting consideration of alternatives.

Some years ago, my book club read *History of Love* by Nicole Krauss. It's a story about the reappearance of a long-lost book that mysteriously connects an old man searching for his son and a girl seeking a cure for her widowed mother's loneliness. The stories intertwine, frequently punctuated with the short phrase, "And yet." The first time I hardly noticed it. Before long, the phrase began jumping out at me, inspiring me to wonder what alternate possibilities could be unfolding.

Ironically, the phrase stuck with me more than the story itself, those two words becoming a refrain daring me to look at things differently.

It's a tool I still use, deliberately adding it to my self-chatter: *seems like I ought to make plans for the holidays. And yet.* (And yet they are months away. What's my rush?) *Life is so difficult right now. And yet.* (And yet I'm tired, bone tired. That's probably the biggest cause of my moroseness.) *Things aren't going well with my current project. And yet.* (And yet I know my rhythm of progress historically tends to run in cycles of productivity alternating with cycles of disorganized dithering while my spirit regroups and my energy rebounds.) And yet!

"And yet" gives me permission. It invites questions and curiosity, those old friends that help sustain traction while going and growing forward. It asks me to check the veracity of my thoughts, which is especially useful since I live alone and have no one to bounce thoughts around with, no one to counter my faulty thinking unless I do so myself.

When in doubt, throw in an "And yet..." and see where that leads.

CARRYING FORWARD VS. MOVING ON

Life is to live. Love is there.
Nothing is a promise,

But beauty exists, and it must
be hunted for and found.

~ Joan Baez

OF ALL the things that people said to me after Jack's death, the most upsetting was "Surely you've moved on . . ." Those words came at me with startling frequency beginning soon (!) after he died and continuing throughout the months and years that followed. I still hear this phrase, now and again.

Any time I heard this, what I wanted to say was, "Who are you to tell me I should 'move on?' How could you possibly know what it is like to have your life totally dismantled in the twinkling of an eye?"

I never said that, however, because even in the midst of my pain I knew that the people saying this meant well, that when they said, "It's time to move on," what they really meant was they wanted me to feel better.

(I sometimes suspect that what they wanted even more—albeit subconsciously—was to feel better *themselves*. Watching others' pain is unsettling. We want to see that pain dissipate because we are afraid of the possibility of our own pain, wondering if we will be able to deal with it. If we see that someone else has "moved on," it encourages us to believe that we will be able to do that as well. No big deal . . .)

Alas, these words were anything but helpful, serving only to sow seeds of failure, the idea that somehow I wasn't doing what I should to put my life back together. I wasn't enough. I didn't do enough.

The idea of "moving on" bothers me, too, because it sounds like something you do when you accidentally run over a woodchuck on the road. It's as if someone I loved was run over, and instead of stopping, I was supposed to simply keep driving onward, leaving them in my dust. The phrase implies a cavalier sense that people are expendable.

The idea is repugnant and disrespectful, but it also doesn't work that way. We don't forget whether we want to or not. The question is *how* to remember, *how* to carry the best part of someone we knew forward with us, not living in the past but not leaving them behind, either. Rather, it's about how to incorporate our history with them into our tomorrows.

There is no one way, no magic formula, but getting rid of the idea that one should "Move On" is a good place to start the painful process of rebuilding an altered life. All that's accomplished by pressure to do something we don't know how to do is the creation of shame, and shame stops all forward motion. Shame is a one-trick pony: the only thing it knows how to do is hide, in this case, hiding imagined inadequacy.

Neither need we wear the mask of "fake amnesia," pretending we've forgotten, because "either-or" is a false construct. When we lose someone, we miss them, *and* we remember them. We hold on to our memories *and* we look for new ways to invest our love and energy. We don't have to abandon the past to be able to go forward. One outlook does not negate the other. It's another case of the "both-and" attitude instead of the "either-or" implied by "moving on."

Life is like a jigsaw puzzle. Over time, we assemble a "big picture" for ourselves by picking up various pieces here and there, working on them, and altering them to fit with other pieces to form a coherent whole. When life feels copacetic, there are no huge gaping holes. When a life-altering experience happens, however, it is as if a tornado blew through and disassembled the puzzle, leaving the pieces lying about like leaves scattered after a storm. I imagine myself, the survivor, in a scene out of the evening news, standing there in a stupor, all semblance of familiar surroundings torn apart and strewn around willy-nilly. "Move on?" How?

The puzzle metaphor suggests a process.

First, look at the pieces—observe them carefully, all of them, wherever they landed—and take in on a gut level that things are forever altered. Some pieces are gone, others tattered and changed. Still others wait patiently to be picked up and resituated in the new configuration.

In time, begin to pick up some pieces (family, friends, activities) and work to rearrange them, incorporating them to form a new whole. Just as with a jigsaw puzzle, you may not pick up the piece you're looking for on the first try. It's an experimental process of trial and error requiring imagination, tenacity, and humor.

Trials that worked for me: renting a cottage in Maine to serve as an alternate "northern woods and water fix," since living on a boat on the St. Lawrence River in the summer was no longer possible. More dinners with friends because there were no longer any "dinners for two." Learning to laugh at my handywoman ineptness rather than cry about it, going to YouTube, following instructional videos to solve problems that used to be outside my sphere of responsibilities, and finding a handyman for those things still beyond my scope.

Trials that didn't work: some of my attempts to join groups in the community. After several of these forays, I remember feeling totally, utterly inept, fifth wheel-like, not fitting in at all, the conversations going on around and beyond me, but not with me. The first time that happened I cried when I got home. The second time I had the presence of spirit to remember that not all things work for all people, and I laughed. *Another one down . . . I wonder what's next.* My "peeps," as my daughter calls them, are out there. I just need to keep reaching out until I find them. It's rare to find what you're looking for with the first stab into the haystack.

Remembering helped me "re-member" and rebuild. It illuminated my path as surely as a lamp shining over the puzzle table. I am part of everyone I've ever known and loved, and they are part of me— unforgettable, inseparable, and in the ultimate sense, forever. Instead of trying to "move on" from them, better to sort through my memories and retrieve the parts that sustain me, the very essence of the one who is no longer at my side. Then I can carry that essence forward with me as I build my new way of living.

The weight of this essence is nothing at all, unlike the weight of shame and "shoulds," which are heavy burdens indeed. Quite the contrary, these memories buoy me for the journey ahead.

Thus, I worked with all the pieces with deliberate intention. I acknowledged the ones that were taken from me and gently let them go. I reshaped some so they could fit together in new ways. I discarded others that no longer fit. I found or created new ones to fill in the gaps. The picture that emerged combined the best of what was with nascent possibilities for a future infused with the essence of the missing piece that I sought to bring along instead of leaving at the side of the road like forgotten roadkill.

In time, I was able to feel the love without dwelling in loss and yesterdays. In time, that love nourished integration of all I have experienced with fresh possibilities to form a new, different kind of cohesion.

I chose to "carry forward" rather than "move on" so I could be whole again.

EACH THING IN
ITS OWN TIME

There is no path that goes all the way.

~ *Han Shan*

AND SO, time passed. Days, weeks, months, and years—time itself a gift that took time to appreciate!

In retrospect, I see how one insight led to another, one experience opened the next, one conundrum and then the next revealed new ways to look at things as possibilities instead of problems.

Did I mention that all this took time?

This very book you have in your hands is a perfect example. I planned to write it over a decade ago. I set aside time for the project. I bought voice-activated software to shorten the process of transcribing notes and journal entries. I assembled materials. I wrote an outline.

Running out of preparation tasks one fine July morning, I sat down at my computer to begin. Immediately, I had a violent physical reaction, a sensation of repulsion and revulsion from head to toe, shivers of prickles, tension, suddenly hot all over. I had never experienced such a visceral response to anything. I didn't recognize myself or my reaction. What was happening? Why was I feeling this way?

Silence.

Then, awareness ascended from a wellspring deep within my spirit: *I do not want to do this!* I didn't know why, but the message was crystal clear.

For once in my life, I didn't ask questions, I didn't push through, I didn't rearrange, I didn't handwring. I laughed. *Well! That's clear. Not sure what I do want to do, but clearly, it's not this!*

I packed up my notes, threw out my outline, and gave no more thought to writing about widowhood.

A few months ago, out of nowhere, a huge *Aha!* popped into my mind. Three days later I had completed an entire outline, and I began to write like a madwoman.

Looking back, I realize that I could not have written this book all those years ago. What could I possibly have said? I had not yet learned what I needed to know to write it. Rather, I was swept up in wishful thinking, imagining that I had figured things out to a point where the hardest parts were behind me. In truth, I was still deep in uncharted territory. I had not yet adequately figured out how to even begin to reassemble my life. I didn't even know that I didn't know.

"I" didn't know I wasn't ready to write, but my body did.

Before I could write, many pieces had to come together, breadcrumb by breadcrumb. Many experiences needed to piggyback on each other. Time needed to pass, wash over me, slow me down, anesthetize shock, and soothe my wounded spirit. Time would settle the pendulum. Time would reveal the way forward *but only when it was ready to do so.*

Awash in grief, it's mighty scary to consider how long the arc of healing will be, but denying this truth only makes the arc longer. Looking it in the eye makes it possible to proactively decide how to *use* time instead of wishing it away.

There are multiple morals to this story:

Listen to your body! It is wise beyond your ability to fathom.

Each thing in its own time. Sheer willpower cannot overcome wrong timing. If the pupa isn't ready, the butterfly cannot emerge.

Trust Grace. It surpasses explanation and rationalization and engenders deep peace, "the peace that passes all understanding." The revelations we are looking for will come, in their own time, their own way, and very likely from an unexpected quarter.

My story is a testament of survival. Hard parts come and go. Over time they are farther and farther apart. Over time I not only survived, but I learned to thrive. You can, too.

CHAPTER EIGHT

FOOTHOLD

[A] great warm wind blew through
and against our backs, as if to blow
away our befores forever, now
that our afters had begun.

~ *Elizabeth von Arnim*

THE MISSING LINK

If we can accept that nothing is permanent,
and change is inevitable, if we can adapt,
then we're going to be happier people.

~ Louise Penny

UNBIDDEN, THE pieces came together.

After fifteen years of seeking wholeness and solid grounding without Jack, never quite able to hit the mark, a sudden understanding popped into my consciousness: *the only place to find true, lasting, enduring belonging is within the Eternal Mystery, the cosmos, God.* (By whatever name one chooses to label this mystery.)

I grasped my error: I had been asking for the impossible, seeking permanence from impermanence. Wanting Jack (or someone or something in his place) to be for me what only the Silent, Mystical Universe in its all-encompassing entirety can be. All other belongings are temporal. Seasons, for sure, but not permanent grounding. That was my Holy Grail, and I was looking for it in the wrong place.

This was not a new thought exactly, but there is intellectual knowing and another, very different kind of knowing—the knowing that is beyond words, felt in the depths of the soul. I sometimes think we are like little children learning about sex: we grasp only what we can understand in the moment. The rest blissfully passes over our heads until we've acquired greater ability to understand.

I grabbed my journal, not wanting to lose this budding insight. How to wrap a frame around the thought of true belonging? It speaks:

I picture Mother Earth. (Indeed, I do think she is a mother! Patient, long-suffering, loving, accepting, adapting.) Mother Earth is all about connections, each thing/person/being a part of the whole, needed to create the whole. The only true grounding we can expect from our time on earth comes from acknowledging and acquiescing to these connections, agreeing to belong, and finally agreeing to accept change when the time for change arrives. Mother Earth holds us—Spirit holds us—but we don't get to make the rules. We get to be held!

What suffering we wreak upon ourselves when we ask for, hope for, and obsess about wanting permanent grounding from impermanent sources! Looking for it from people who, like us, are here for an indeterminate period, their timetables generally failing to align with our own.

And so, we must let these loved ones go! Release them to their next chapters unburdened by our agendas and expectations.

*Of course, we have no idea what engages their spirits. It is not ours to know. The important shift takes place in **us**. Freed from our agendas, we can begin to embrace our changed lives with eyes wide open for other connections that await us. Possibilities will abound if we allow them to evolve.*

I am astonished by what "the pen" knows, insights that pour forth when I simply write by hand, bodily engagement somehow key to unlocking truths when they are ready to come forth.

Letting loved ones go does not mean forgetting them. We carry the best of those we love forward with us in our hearts, in our very ways of being. But they do not, they cannot, "ground" us. The mistake is thinking they ever did. Only life itself is large enough to ground us.

Nature is full of examples of groundings and connections. Aspen groves with root systems under the surface that interreact and support each other. The eternal coming and going of the tides, the waxing and waning of the moon, the passing of seasons, the constant cycle of death making way for new life. Eternal rhythms and divine harmonies surround us. Our job is to tune into them and be willing to join the dance. That's how we get to be part of this gigantic miracle!

On a roll, I explored other analogies, starting with Hansel and Gretel. I picture them, Hansel in his lederhosen, Gretel in her dirndl, clasping hands for courage as they tentatively explore the forest.

I question my journal:

> *So what happens when Hansel dies?*
>
> *Gretel must revise her way of thinking. She must come to realize that Hansel's extended hand is not the only one she will ever experience. And in times like this, she must, in the words of poet David Wagoner,*
>
> *"Stand still. The trees ahead and bushes beside you are not lost. Wherever you are is called Here.... The forest knows where you are. You must let it find you."*
>
> *The forest: metaphor for the entirety. The* **entirety** *is my grounding, my anchor, not a single hand, no matter how precious. Do I miss that extended hand? Of course I do! I always will. But life is larger than any one hand, any one connection, even such a beloved one.*

In that moment I felt my spirit shift. I felt cracked open, changed. Loneliness not dispelled, exactly, but incorporated in a different way. Loneliness as my teacher, as a friend, not an enemy. So many new ideas to explore, Curiosity lighting the way forward.

* * *

And yet. All good and fine, high-minded, Pollyanna Bright Side . . . but I can't cuddle up to enlightenment in the dark of night. I want this new glimmer of understanding to endure, to be able to withstand inevitable gloomy interludes. I want staying power. I want to put this shift in perception into practice.

"Practice" is the linchpin. My frame of mind and spirit will be a work in progress until I take my last breath. There will be enlightened, upbeat, optimistic times but also dark nights of the soul, times when the light dims, when courage flags, when simple longing cannot be denied. It's not a case of either-or but rather of both-and.

C.S. Lewis, who knew a thing or two about grief, wrote about the importance of practice: "Relying on God has to begin all over again every day as if nothing had yet been done." It's not a once-and-done thing; it's about being ready to make yet another effort, to start over again and again. To be present to whatever shows up, grateful to be alive, alert, and aware, asking, *What is in this moment?*

If no magic wand can waft away the bouts of emptiness, then I must acknowledge and allow them. I cannot tilt the scale toward larger belonging unless I consent to the presence of the dark side when it decides to show up. Questioning is my best recourse. *Darkness: What would you teach me? I want to learn to see you as friend, not foe, the forerunner of returning light, for light always reappears after darkness.*

Acting with intention, I consent to the entirety—the best of my yesterdays, the hardships of today, my doubts about tomorrows. I will let the past be the past, but I will also allow myself to be buoyed by the memories of those I love who are no longer here on earth. I will carry them forward with me on this great adventure in the forest. I will trust that Light will prevail.

We human beings have limited sight when overwhelmed by shock, sorrow, and scary changes in circumstances. We slip into self-criticism, expecting more of ourselves than our present levels of understanding can deliver. We need the warmth of self-compassion. Kindness opens us in ways that self-flagellation never will.

Underneath it all, around it all, over it all, through it all, we are held. We are part of a plan that is bigger than any one of us, and that ... THAT ... is grounding.

I will go forward, then, "trusting the slow work of God." *(Pierre Teilhard de Chardin)*

I don't know where I'm going
But I'm on my way.

~ *Voltaire*

RESOURCES

So many books, so little time!

AS A reader, I turned to books and online research to guide my path as I grieved. Although the following list could be much longer, I include only the books and other resources that were the most helpful to me during my journey of healing following loss.

Early On:

- Hickman, Martha Whitmore. *Healing After Loss: Daily Meditations for Working Through Grief.* 1st ed. New York: William Morrow Paperbacks, 1994.

  A classic, and a treasure: a little book of daily readings that contain a quote from literature, the Bible, or wisdom traditions, followed by a brief meditation about the quote, ending with an affirmation. For example, "I have some control over how much I let sadness rule my life." I found it helpful in the early days following loss.

- Chödrön, Pema. *When Things Fall Apart: Heart Advice for Difficult Times.* Boston: Shambala, 1997.

  "Pema Chodron is one of those spiritual teachers who brings ancient wisdom to bear upon our daily triumphs and tragedies . . . . Incredibly wise and poignantly practical." —Spirituality & Health

- Stillwater, Michael, and Malkin, Gary. *Graceful Passages: A Companion for Living and Dying.* (A book and two-CD set.) Novato: New World Library, 2003.

  A beautiful little book that includes contributions from many traditions, with entries written by noted authors Kübler-Ross, Ram Dass, Thich Nhat Hanh, Rabbin Zalman Schachter-Shalomi, Ira Byock, MD, and others. On one of the accompanying CDs, the entries are read aloud to background music. The other, the music by itself, is what I listened to day after day during the first year after my husband died. Quiet, plaintive, and intuitive, it somehow called me to an acceptance of sorts.

- Lewis, C. S. *A Grief Observed.* 1st ed. New York: HarperOne, 2015.

  Another classic with honest reflections on the fundamental issues of life, death, and faith in the midst of loss.

Exploring the Grief Process:

- Bonanno, George A. *The Other Side of Sadness: What the New Science of Bereavement Tells Us About Life After Loss.* New York: Basic Books, 2009.

  "Bonanno carefully assembles scientific evidence to show that most of what we thought we knew is just plain wrong. If you want to know the truth about the human experience of loss, there's only one book on the shelf." —Daniel Gilbert, professor of psychology, Harvard University.

- Kübler-Ross, Elisabeth. *On Death and Dying: What the Dying Have to Teach Doctors, Nurses, Clergy and Their Own Families.* Reissue ed., New York: Scribner, 2014.

  One of the most important psychological studies of the late twentieth century, On Death and Dying *grew out of Dr. Kübler-Ross's famous interdisciplinary seminar on death, life, and transition.*

- Kübler-Ross, Elisabeth. *On Grief and Grieving: Finding the Meaning of Grief Through the Five Stages of Loss.* Reprint ed. New York: Scribner, 2014.

  An adaptation of Kübler-Ross's theories on the death and dying stages of grieving.

- Berger, Susan A. *The Five Ways We Grieve: Finding Your Personal Path to Healing after the Loss of a Loved One.* Reprint ed. Boston: Trumpeter, 2011.

  Berger goes beyond the commonly held theories of the stages of grief. She offers hope with a plan—in the form of new ways to recognize, define, and focus on our changed identity and worldview after loss.

- Nepo, Mark: *Falling Down and Getting Up: Discovering Your Inner Resilience and Strength.* New York: St. Martin's Publishing Group, 2023

  "Amid this luminous new collection of wisdom, Mark Nepo offers one of the most robust and tender teachings on grief I have come across. In Mark's hands, pain becomes poetry, and enlarges our hearts enough to carry what we may have thought we couldn't." —Mirabai Starr

- Edelman, Hope. *The AfterGrief: Finding Your Way Along the Long Arc of Loss.* New York: Ballentine, 2020.

  Another book offering a viewpoint beyond grieving regarded as stages. Edelman's book is a validating new approach to the long-term grieving process that explains why we feel "stuck," why that's normal, and how shifting our perception of grief can help us grow.

- Kessler, David. *Finding Meaning: The Sixth Stage of Grief.* New York: Scribner, 2020.

  "The pain of grief is a natural reaction to the loss of someone you love. But . . . suffering 'is what our minds do

to us,' and it can be mitigated by finding meaning in what we've lost." —Jane Brody, The New York Times.

- Levine, Stephen. *Unattended Sorrow: Recovering from Loss and Reviving the Heart.* 2nd ed. Boston: Monkfish Book Publishing, 2019.

  Wise, compassionate advice from one of the nation's most trusted grief counselors to help heal emotional wounds that prevent us from leading fulfilling lives.

Emotions:

- Brown, Brené. *Atlas of the Heart: Mapping Meaningful Connection and the Language of Human Experience.* New York: Random House, 2021.

  Don't be intimidated by the lofty title. This is a reference book to have on your shelf, a book to turn to when your emotions are in a muddle. Brown explores groups of emotions in depth and helps readers to sort out how to understand and deal with them.

- Lerner, Harriet, PhD. *The Dance of Anger: A Woman's Guide to Changing the Patterns of Intimate Relationships.* Reprint ed. New York: William Morrow Paperbacks, 2014.

  "Anger is a signal and one worth listening to," writes Lerner. A helpful book for sorting out how to understand and deal with this emotion.

- Lerner, Harriet, PhD. *Fear and Other Uninvited Guests: Tackling the Anxiety, Fear, and Shame That Keep Us from*

Optimal Living and Loving. New York: HarperCollins, 2004.

Another helpful book from Lerner. Easy to read, relate to, and understand. Presents useful strategies for breaking free from fear.

- Greenspan, Miriam. *Healing Through the Dark Emotions: The Wisdom of Grief, Fear, and Despair.* Boston: Shambala, 2003.

Important, in-depth look at grief, fear, and despair. Greenspan argues that these emotions are not harmful but have redemptive power. When embraced, we can use them to turn our pain into wisdom and our fear and sorrow into positive energy.

- Viorst, Judith. *Necessary Losses: The Loves, Illusions, Dependencies and Impossible Expectations that All of Us Have to Give Up in Order to Grow.* New York: Simon & Schuster, 1998.

Viorst examines loss as an integral part of living. Accepting the loss of our loved ones through separation and death, we can gain deeper perspective, true maturity, and fuller wisdom about life. Useful when wondering, "Why did this have to happen?"

Loneliness and Solitude:

- Falk, Florence. *On My Own: The Art of Being a Woman Alone.* New York: Three Rivers Press, 2007.

  "Florence Falk's On My Own *is a provocative, smart read for any woman who is alone, wants to be alone, or is figuring out how to be alone. An empowering, emotionally honest book that is long overdue." —Amy Sohn, author.*

- Brown, Brené. *Braving the Wilderness: The Quest for True Belonging and the Courage to Stand Alone.* Reprint ed. New York: Random House Trade Paperbacks, 2019.

  Very helpful for evaluating how we think about ourselves and what it means to belong. Especially useful when self-definition has been torn asunder. Brown's works are unfailingly accessible and hopeful.

- Iyer, Pico. *The Art of Stillness: Adventures in Going Nowhere.* New York: TED Books, Simon & Schuster, 2014.

  Iyer is known for his writings about traveling and cultures, seemingly contradictory to stillness. Here he states the case for going slow and paying attention. "Nothing," he says, "is more urgent than sitting still." A manifesto for accepting solitude, I found his thesis key to redefining loneliness.

- Sarton, May. *Journal of a Solitude.* First ed. New York: W. W. Norton & Company, 1977.

  A raw, honest look at the ups and downs of learning (or relearning) to be alone. "Loneliness is the poverty of self; solitude is richness of self." —May Sarton

Daybooks to Inspire and Light the Way Forward:

Most of the following books were not specifically designed to be daybooks, but I have found using them as such offers me one kernel of encouragement at a time as I start a new day.

- Nepo, Mark. *The Book of Awakening: Having the Life You Want by Being Present to the Life You Have.* San Francisco: Conari Press, 2000. (Newer editions available)

  My daughter gave me a copy of this shortly after my husband died. The title captures its essence—poignant counsel for the newly bereaved. Nepo has a gift for metaphor and analogy, suggesting lessons we can learn from everyday objects and experiences. He has written many other books, all of them poetic and remarkable, but this one feels like the gold standard, the one I return to year after year.

- Smith, Maggie. *Keep Moving: Notes on Loss, Creativity, and Change.* New York: One Signal Publishers, 2020.

  A gem! Every entry ends with "Keep Moving," and this book will help you do so.

- Strayed, Cheryl. *Brave Enough.* New York: Alfred A. Knopf, 2015.

  A book of memorable quotes from Strayed's writings. Pithy, direct, with humor, grit, and courage laced throughout. Especially upbeat and encouraging.

- Bayda, Ezra. *Saying Yes to Life (Even the Hard Parts).* Boston: Wisdom Publications, 2005.

  Chapters with short notes on everything from "The Human Dilemma" to "Who We Truly Are." As Thomas Moore states in the introduction, "Like all good Zen writing, it pulls the rug out from under your most cherished truths and habits . . . " cleaning the slate as you reconfigure your way of being.

- Cameron, Julia. *Transitions: Prayers and Declarations for a Changing Life.* New York: Putnam, 1999.

  Reassuring, short meditations on change and changing.

- Lasater, Judith Hanson. *A Year of Living Your Yoga: Daily Practices to Shape Your Life.* Berkeley: Rodmell Press, 2006.

  No practice of yoga required to benefit from this book, which offers a brief thought a day for consideration. It is direct, kind, and motivating.

Books for Personal Growth and Healing the Soul:

- Licata, Matt, PhD. *A Healing Space: Befriending Ourselves in Difficult Times.* Boulder: Sounds True, 2020.

  If you choose only one book about healing, choose this one! Lauded by therapists, poets, spiritual gurus, and clinical psychologists, this book is in a class by itself. Warm, accessible, reassuring. It will envelop you in possibility and peace.

- Cain, Susan. *Bittersweet: How Sorrow and Longing Make Us Whole.* New York: Crown, 2022.

  "What is sadness good for?" asks Cain. A thoughtful meditation on the complicated relationships and interactions among our histories, feelings, creativities, and desires to create legacies. Culminates with meditations on Mortality, Impermanence, and Grief. Surprisingly affirming and soothing.

- Singer, Michael A. *The Untethered Soul: The Journey Beyond Yourself.* Oakland: New Harbinger Publications, 2007.

- Singer, Michael A. *Living Untethered: Beyond the Human Predicament.* Oakland: New Harbinger Publications, 2022.

  "True personal growth is about transcending the part of you that is not okay and needs protection," says Singer.

His books explore how we think about ourselves, how we can let go of what we've outgrown, and how we can go beyond into new ways of being.

- O'Donohue, John. *Walking on the Pastures of Wonder (in Conversation with John Quinn).* Dublin: Veritas, 2015.

A book of great insight and riches, presented in O'Donohue's inimitable, lyrical style, addressing many of the issues faced by bereaved people: loneliness, absence, balance, and aging. A treasure.

- Frankl, Viktor E. *Man's Search for Meaning.* Boston: Beacon Press, 1959.

Frankl was a Holocaust survivor. He lost everything— everything!—but refused to lose hope. He argues that we cannot avoid suffering, but we can choose how to cope with it, find meaning in it, and move forward with renewed purpose. A book to restore your perspective when you lose sight of meaning.

- Palmer, Parker J. *A Hidden Wholeness: The Journey Toward An Undivided Life.* San Francisco: Jossey-Bass, 2004.

Palmer has much to say about living with integrity. Here, he speaks to our yearning to live undivided lives—lives that are congruent with our inner truth—in a world filled with the forces of fragmentation.

- Palmer, Parker J. *Let Your Life Speak: Listening for the Voice of Vocation.* San Francisco: Jossey-Bass, 2000.

  Here, Palmer writes about learning to listen to the teacher within, follow its lead toward a sense of meaning and purpose. Helpful when in the midst of redefining a life after loss.

- Palmer, Parker J. *On the Brink of Everything: Grace, Gravity & Getting Old.* Oakland: Berrett-Koehler Publishers, 2018.

  "A brave and beautiful book for all who want to age reflectively, seeking new insights and life-giving ways to engage the world," from quote on book jacket. Affirming and thought-provoking.

In a Class by Themselves:

I am grateful to have these two books on my shelf to refer to when I'm not quite sure what I need or how I'm feeling. In both cases, I turn to the table of contents and see what seems to draw me in. Very helpful!

- O'Donohue, John. *To Bless the Space Between Us: A Book of Blessings.* New York: Doubleday, 2008.

  A compelling blend of elegant, poetic language and spiritual insight that offers comfort and encouragement to readers on their journeys through life. Entries address everything from Thresholds to Desires to States of the

Heart to Beyond Endings. Reassuring, calming, and inspiring.

- Whyte, David. *Consolations: The Solace, Nourishment and Underlying Meaning of Everyday Words.* Langley, Washington: Many Rivers Press, 2015.

  Individual essays on common words, starting with Alone and ending with Work, with many entries in between that will change the way you look at things, including Anger, Despair, Heartbreak, Hope, Loneliness, Naming, Silence, and Solace. A treasure!

Inspirations:

- Tolle, Eckhart, and McDonnell, Patrick. *Guardians of Being.* Novato: New World Library, 2009.

  A creative collaboration between spiritual teacher Tolle and MUTTS comic strip writer McDonnell. A ten-minute read that reminds us to slow down, stop thinking, and be. I pick it up when I need an infusion of simplicity and energy.

- Sacks, Oliver. *Gratitude.* New York: Knopf, 2015.

  "A series of heart-rending yet ultimately uplifting essays .... A lasting gift to readers .... unlike other writers who have reported from the front lines of mortality, Sacks did not focus on his illness, his medical ordeal or spirituality, but on 'what is meant by living a good and worthwhile life—achieving a sense of peace within oneself.'" —Heller McAlpin, The Washington Post

- Lama, Dalai, and Tutu, Desmond. *The Book of Joy.* New York: Avery, 2016.

  Just what its title implies: conversations between two spiritual giants on finding joy amid tribulation. Uplifting.

- Nerburn, Kent. *Small Graces: The Quiet Gifts of Everyday Life.* Novato: New World Library, 1998.

  In this as well as in his other equally lovely "little books," Nerburn invites readers to slow down and observe the everyday blessings of our lives, even amid sorrows or traumas.

- Gibran, Kahlil. *The Prophet.* New York: Knopf, 1961.

  Gibran's beloved classic contains essays on many states of being human, including love, joy and sorrow, freedom, beauty, pain, self-knowledge, and death. A book to refer to in times of seeking.

- Rogers, Fred. *The World According to Mister Rogers: Important Things to Remember.* New York: Hyperion, 2003.

  An inspiring collection of stories, anecdotes, and insights told in Mister Rogers' simple, kind, unassuming voice. Tonic for the soul!

Anthologies of Quotes:

- Safransky, Sy. *Sunbeams: A Book of Quotations.*
  Berkeley: North Atlantic Books, 1990.

  A collection of the best Sunbeams from the early years of
  The Sun *magazine. An incredible collection of thoughts.*
  Although not directly categorized, similar ideas are
  grouped together between lines of circles. Incisive gems—
  worth the trouble to find them.

- Safransky, Sy. *Paper Lanterns: More Quotations from*
  the Back Pages of The Sun. Chapel Hill: The Sun
  Publishing Company, 2010.

  "Unlike the earlier collection, there is an order to the
  quotations in Paper Lanterns *which takes us on a*
  journey through innocence and experience, love and loss,
  disillusionment and awakening." (from the introduction)

- Branch, Susan. *Distilled Genius: The Illustrated Secrets*
  of Life. A Collection of Life-Changing Quotations.
  Martha's Vineyard: Spring Street Publishing, 2022.

  A quirky, wonderful collection of quotes handwritten
  and illustrated by the author, organized by topics such as
  Quiet, Friendship, Dark Clouds: Breaking Up, Sadness,
  Broken Hearts, Starting Over, and Courage and Faith.
  Lovely to pick up and dip into at random.

Poetry:

- Crews, James, Editor. *How to Love the World: Poems of Gratitude and Hope.* North Adams: Storey Publishing, 2021.

  "Joy is the happiness that doesn't depend on what happens." —Brother David Steindl-Rast. A book of collected poems to leaven even the darkest days.

- Oliver, Mary. *Thirst.* Boston: Beacon Press, 2006.

  Thirst *contains poems Oliver wrote as she grappled with grief at the death of her beloved partner.*

In addition to the many wonderful books of poetry by Oliver, other poets I turn to are Barbara Crooker, David Whyte, T.S. Eliot, Rumi, Billy Collins, Hafiz, Wendell Berry, Tony Hoagland, Robert Frost, e e cummings, Marge Piercy, and Linda Pastan, among so many others. Poems get at truth sideways, somehow articulating something metaphorically or descriptively that you already knew deep down in your bones. I try to read at least one poem a day.

Books of Fiction, Essays, and Memoirs:

- Didion, Joan. *The Year of Magical Thinking.* New York: Knopf, 2005.

  A searing account of experiencing sudden loss. Unforgettable.

- Godwin, Gail: Novels including *Evensong, Old Lovegood Girls, Grief Cottage,* and *Father Melancholy's Daughter.*

  Godwin's novels never disappoint—there is always a connection between her stories and characters and the life issues I am dealing with.

- Taylor, Barbara Brown. *An Altar in the World: A Geography of Faith.* New York: HarperOne, 2009.

  "Taylor shares how she learned to find God beyond the church walls by embracing the sacred as a natural part of everyday life. Through her guidance and delicate, thought-provoking prose, we learn to live with purpose, pay attention, slow down, and revere the world we live in." (from quote on book cover)

- Roth, Geneen. *The Craggy Hole in My Heart and The Cat Who Fixed It.* New York: Three Rivers Press, 2004.

  Offbeat, surprising, and ultimately joyous book about grief and healing involving lessons from Mister Blanche, Roth's cat.

- Lamott, Anne: Six remarkable books of essays:

  Help Thanks Wow: The Three Essential Prayers
  Stitches: A Handbook on Meaning, Hope, and Repair
  Hallelujah Anyway: Rediscovering Mercy
  Almost Everything: Notes on Hope
  Small Victories: Spotting Improbable Moments of Grace
  Dusk Night Dawn: On Revival and Courage

All published by Riverhead Books, New York, between 2012 and 2021.

Basically, if Anne Lamott writes a book, I read it. She is smart, funny, and tells it like it is with heart, humor, imagination, humility, and hope. You can't go wrong with Anne Lamott.

Websites for Reference:

- Gwen Suesse: https://gwensuesseauthor.com/

  Information about Gwen and her books.

- Act 2 Life Coaching: https://act2lifecoaching.com/

  Information about Gwen's coaching practice, as well as a link to her blog, Now It's Time to Dance.

- Creative Grief Studio: https://creativegriefstudio.com/ what-is-the-creative-grief-studio/

  This is the organization under which I trained for grief support certification. For self-study possibilities, check out: https://creativegriefstudio.com/five-new-self-study-courses/

- Grief Rejection Resilience: A Mash-up: https:// mintchipstudios.com/blog/grief-rejection-resilience

  This is an entry from my daughter's (Jennifer Stine) leadership coaching website. She includes a powerful set of thoughts, poetry, images, and essays. Don't miss it!

- Grief Support for the Rest of Us: https://whatsyourgrief.
  com/

  *Wealth of resources related to grieving, including
  a powerful graphic about growing around grief:*
  https://whatsyourgrief.com/growing-around-grief/

Websites Concerning Suicide:

- https://www.cnet.com/health/suicide-hotlines-crisis-hotlines-to-call-when-you-need-help/

- https://save.org/find-help/

- https://www.mayoclinic.org/diseases-conditions/
  suicide/in-depth/suicide/art-20044707

---

*If you are having suicidal thoughts, do
not wait—seek help immediately!*

ACKNOWLEDGMENTS

My daughter, Jennifer Stine, and my son, Ned Suesse—linking past, present, and future with affirmations of support, wisdom, humor, and love. My path forward after loss is unimaginable without your abiding presence. I'm thankful to be blessed with such stellar offspring!

Marsha Van Hecke—kindred spirit, friend, confidant, first reader, sister writer, and editor *par excellence.* My writing is sharper because of your spot-on suggestions. No words are adequate to express my gratitude and love.

Tricia Orcutt—visionary graphic artist, designer, and friend. You make my ideas look good! You're always a step ahead of me with the perfect creative approach, not to mention how much fun we have together in the process.

Deb Phillips—counselor extraordinaire. Wise, caring, and funny, you always (and I do mean *always*) come up with the right thought or idea to nudge me forward. I am greatly blessed to have your guidance.

Kathy Willis—friend for fifty-four years and counting . . . Ever present and quietly encouraging with an uncanny ability to offer the exact idea needed at key times during my writing adventures. Neither of my books would have happened without you. Truly!

Audio Angelica—sisterhood of singers and friends. Or is it friends and singers? All those gatherings—singing, feasting, and carousing together . . . You add so much joy to my life.

Beloved Tryon community—my adopted home, like no other place on earth. Thank you, Tryon, for all the ways you've kept me glued together and been my "chosen family."

Finally, a tip of my hat to myriad others who helped this book come into being—authors I know only through their writings. Editors and book mavens. Friends and professional colleagues. Coaching connections. So many kind people too numerous to name . . . You know who you are, and so do I! Thank you.

ABOUT THE AUTHOR

AFTER ACQUIRING a bachelor of arts degree from Wagner College, Gwen earned a master of arts in teaching degree from Harvard University. She is a certified Martha Beck Life Coach, certified by the Creative Grief Studio as a Creative Grief Support Practitioner, and certified as an administrator of the Myers-Briggs Type Inventory. Gwen has broad history of professional experience, including teaching, choral conducting, working in human resources, life coaching, leading volunteer organizations, writing, and conducting workshops. She has presented keynotes at women's conferences, book clubs, and charity events.

Gwen has lived the modern woman's conundrums. Her first book, *Womansong: Balance and Harmony in a Feminine Key*, was the natural outgrowth of her struggle to accommodate the patriarchal identity of her youth with the growing awareness in her adulthood that women are entitled to their own dreams and self-realization. The book addresses her quest to find a way to balance family, professional, and personal goals. *Womansong* won two awards, taking First Place in Women's Issues in the Indie Excellence Contest, and tying for Bronze in the Ippy Awards Contest.

Her second book, *Notes from Planet Widow: Finding My Way After Loss*, picks up her story years later, after the unexpected death of her beloved husband landed her in the alien territory of widowhood. It recounts how a trail of insights knit themselves together to restore her sense of wholeness within the altered context of being on her own.

Active in the communities she's been pleased to call home, Gwen served on a board of education and on numerous boards of community nonprofit organizations, including as president of Tryon Concert Association for fifteen years. She lives in Tryon, North Carolina, in the foothills of the Blue Ridge Mountains.

Made in United States
North Haven, CT
12 September 2024